The Route of the Cornish Riviera Express

London Paddington to Penzance

This book is dedicated to my family and friends.

Copyright © Alexander J. Naughton 2026

All Rights Reserved

No part of this publication may be reproduced, distributed, or transmitted in any form or by any means, including photocopying, recording, or other electronic or mechanical methods, without the author's prior written permission, except in the case of brief quotations embodied in critical reviews and certain other non-commercial uses permitted by copyright law. For permission requests, please get in touch with the author.

Contents

- Acknowledgements: i
- About the Author ii
- Introduction 2
- **Route Description** **14**
  - London Paddington to Reading: 19
  - Reading to Taunton: 23
  - Taunton to Exeter St Davids: 35
  - Exeter St Davids to Plymouth: 43
  - Plymouth to Penzance: 62
- **THE NIGHT RIVIERA SLEEPER** **95**
  - (London Paddington to Penzance) 95
- **The Destinations** **106**
  - Penzance 106
  - St. Ives 112
  - Falmouth 117
  - Truro 123
  - Fowey 124
  - Newquay 129
  - Looe 132
  - Padstow 136
  - The Lizard 142
  - Land's End 146
- **Cornwall's Walking Trails** **150**
- **References:** **153**
- **Image Information:** **154**

Acknowledgements:

Writing a book is a complex and time consuming task, so I would like to thank my family and friends for their support and encouragement. The majority of the photos in the book are from my own collections, but for the historic archive photos and travel posters I would like to thank the Science Museum Group's Science & Society Picture Library (https://www.scienceandsociety.co.uk/), Network Rail (https://www.networkrail.co.uk/), Colour Rail (https://colourrail.co.uk/), Alamy (www.alamy.com) and Great Western Railway (https://www.gwr.com/) for their assistance and use of these images.

Lastly I would thank Sara Taylor (Senior Book Publishing and Marketing Consultant), Helen Cooper (Project Manager), the marketing team and the editorial team at Savvy Book Marketing in Liverpool for their expertise, knowledge and professionalism in helping with the graphic design, social media and website aspects as well as their help in editing and formatting the book so that it can be published, put on retail platforms and printed on demand. They have been a great help.

About the Author

I have over 20 years of experience working professionally in local government in the UK, involved in strategic policy & strategy and devolution with a particular focus on placemaking, transport, climate, environment and nature policy, and have a good understanding of the public sector framework and regularly liaise and collaborate with academia and the private and voluntary sectors.

I have valuable skills, including strategy development, big picture strategic thinking, global trends and horizon scanning, innovation, spatial planning, placemaking, product development, marketing, transport & mobility, etc. I have the ability to think holistically and collaboratively through an ambition-led "vision and validate" approach informed by evidence and data. Key thing is to take a holistic, inclusive, place, and whole economy approach to the future of transport to create better places and healthier lives for everyone. I am keen to foster collaboration, engagement and a community enabling approach.

My personal interests include transport, photography, architecture & design, etc. I am also a transport author with this series of "Through the Window" Rail Guides. I strongly believe that, today, with the hectic pace of modern life, technology at our fingertips, and everyone all too often glued to their smartphones, we risk forgetting the simple pleasures of looking out of the window and enjoying slow travel to experience our surroundings.

These "Through the Window" Rail Guides aim to recapture something of this lost art of travel and encourage people to take time to look out of the window to see the passing places, history, culture, landscapes and natural wonders from the train. I see a train journey as linking a string of pearls and showcasing places you pass as well as the destinations you are travelling to. So I hope you enjoy my endeavours!

Introduction

Introduction

Today with the hectic pace of modern life, technology at our fingertips and everyone all too often glued to their smartphones we risk forgetting the simple pleasures of looking out of the window and enjoying slow travel to experience our surroundings. It is good to take a moment to step back, reflect and enjoy life. Take a break from your stressful lives, centre yourself and consider your health & wellbeing. Get out there to explore and discover the sights, sounds and experiences across the country.

These "Through the Window" Travel Guides aim to recapture something of this lost art of travel and encourage people to take time to look out of the window to see the passing places, history, culture, landscapes and natural wonders from the train. We see a train journey as linking a string of pearls and showcasing places you pass as well as the destinations you are travelling to. Look around you and admire some of the wonderful railway architecture to be found in the UK. Take a trip to the seaside for a relaxing dip or meet up with friends for a vibrant city break or simply get back to nature and enjoy some lovely walks in the countryside. So sit back, relax and enjoy your rail journey through Great Britain and its wonderful places and landscapes.

This book focusses on the route from London Paddington to Penzance via the Great Western Main Line. This route was made famous by the Cornish Riviera Express introduced in 1904 by the Great Western Railway. The name was chosen through a public competition in the Railway Magazine, the prize being three guineas (£3.15). Among the 1,286 entries were two suggestions, The Cornish Riviera Limited and The Riviera Express, which were combined as The Cornish Riviera Express. The publicity by the GWR in the 1930s was legendary and created the Holiday Line and the coastal resorts of Cornwall became defined as the Cornish Riviera.

The service was hauled by steam locomotives such as the City, Star, Castle and King class locomotives until 1958 when diesel locomotives were introduced such as the Class 41 Warships, Class 42 Warships, Class 52 Westerns diesel hydraulics and the Class 50 Hoovers and Class 47 diesel locomotives. In 1981 the Intercity 125 High Speed Trains were introduced onto the service and continued until replaced in 2018 by the Hitachi IEP Class 802 bi-mode trains. The service continues today under the privatised railways and is now operated by the Great Western Railway.

In late 2027, the newly nationalised Great British Railways (GBR) will take over the operation of most of Britain's passenger train services, stations, and infrastructure, except for devolved train operators, open-access train operators, and local tram and light rail services.

Devolved train operators include Merseyrail, Transport for London, Scottish Rail Holdings (including ScotRail and Caledonian Sleeper), Transport for Wales, and Translink NI. Open-access operators include Lumo, Hull Trains, Grand Central Rail, and Eurostar.

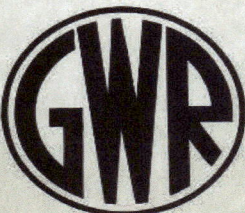

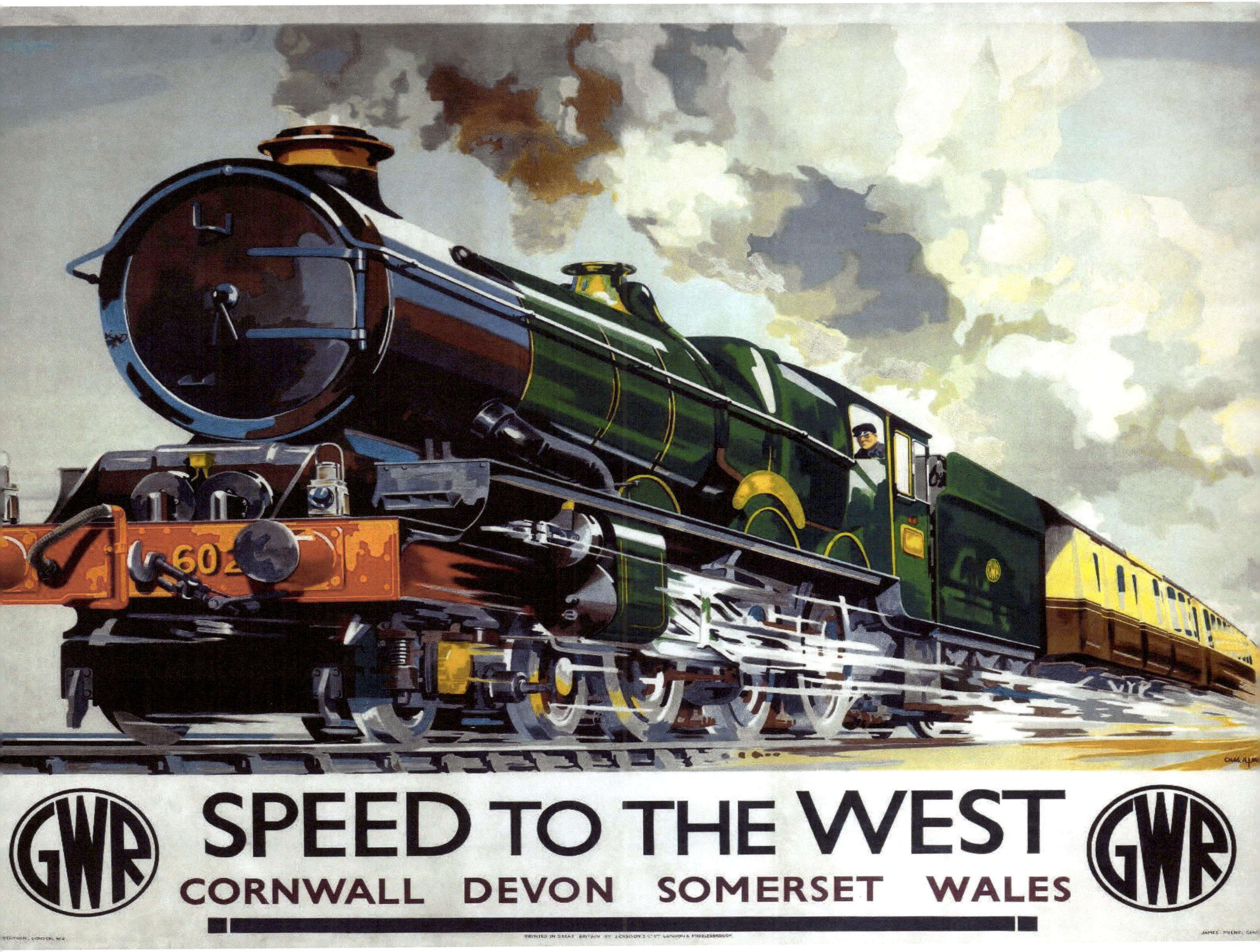
GWR
SPEED TO THE WEST
CORNWALL DEVON SOMERSET WALES
GWR

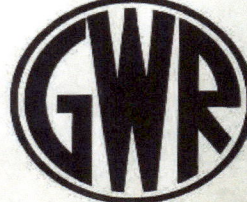

The destination is of course Cornwall. This ancient county and royal duchy is at the far south west of England and is home to Land's End (the westernmost point of Great Britain) and the Lizard (the southernmost point of Great Britain). In medieval times Cornwall was divided into a series of ancient districts known as "hundreds". The original hundreds were Penwith, Kerrier, Pydar, Powder, East and West Wivel and Trigg. The Duchy of Cornwall is held by the Prince of Wales as Duke of Cornwall. It is one of only two remaining Royal Duchies in the UK along with the Duchy of Lancaster. The Duchy of Cornwall remains a major landowner in Cornwall. The Great Western Main Line on its journey through Cornwall forms a spine along the county with wonderful branch lines once diverging from it to coastal resorts such as Newquay, Looe, Falmouth, Padstow, Fowey and St Ives. The surviving branch lines are now marketed as the Great Scenic Railways of Devon & Cornwall. By train you enter Cornwall with the famed crossing of the Royal Albert Bridge at Saltash over the River Tamar. The capital of Cornwall is Truro. Penzance marks the terminus of the Great Western Main Line and has ferry service to the Isles of Scilly further to the south west of Cornwall out in the Atlantic Ocean.

Traditionally the county has been famous for its copper, tin and china clay mining. Today mining is re-emerging in Cornwall with companies such as Cornish Lithium and British Lithium. In the 20th century with the arrival of the railways, tourism became a major industry for the county. Surfing is now very popular on the north coast of Cornwall in resorts such as Newquay and Bude. More recently a major tourist attraction was created near St Austell which is the Eden Project in a former china clay pit. Rick Stein has reinvented Padstow as a culinary hotspot due to his fame as a celebrity TV chef. Also Cornwall has a strong artistic and cultural tradition with hotspots in Newlyn and St Ives. There are strong associations with literature and TV dramas such as Poldark, Rosamund Pilcher and Daphne du Maurier. The late Poet Laureate Sir John Betjeman was famously fond of Cornwall and it featured prominently in his poetry. He is buried in the churchyard at St Enodoc's Church, Trebetherick near Padstow.

In the UK our most outstanding natural landscapes which are highly valued for their unrivalled beauty are designated as either National Parks or National Landscapes, and Cornwall is proud to have a number of National Landscapes including:

Cornwall National Landscape
https://cornwall-landscape.org/

Isles of Scilly National Landscape
https://islesofscilly-nl.org.uk/

Tamar Valley National Landscape
https://www.tamarvalley-nl.org.uk/

Cornwall has a long history in telecommunications and is the landing point for 22 of the world's fastest high-speed undersea and transatlantic fibre optic cables, making Cornwall an important hub within Europe's telecommunication infrastructure. Porthcurno has a strong heritage in the telecommunications industry starting back with the arrival of the first undersea telegraph cable in 1870. Goonhilly Earth Station also has an important role in tracking satellites and Newquay Airport is now a Spaceport as Spaceport Cornwall with a growing role in the space industry.

The Duchy of Cornwall:

The Duchy of Cornwall is a private estate of the Duke of Cornwall, a title which is held by the British monarch's eldest son - the Prince of Wales. The Prince of Wales has a number of titles granted automatically as eldest son including: Duke of Cornwall, Earl of Chester, Duke of Rothesay, Earl of Carrick, Baron Renfrew, Lord of the Isles and Great Steward of Scotland.

The Duchy was established on 17 March 1337 by the Royal Great Charter out of the former Earldom of Cornwall by King Edward III for his son, Edward, Prince of Wales, the "Black Prince", who became the first Duke of Cornwall. The Duchy also exercises certain legal rights and privileges across Cornwall and the Isles of Scilly. The Duke appoints a number of officials in the county and acts as the port authority for the main St Mary's Harbour of the Isles of Scilly. Today its landholdings are centred on particularly Cornwall, Isles of Scilly, Devon, Dorset, Herefordshire and Somerset. In August 1980 the Highgrove estate was purchased by the Duchy of Cornwall. In 1988, West Dorset District Council allocated land in the ducal estate, west of Dorchester, for housing development, which became known as Poundbury. In 2006, Llwynywermod was purchased by the Duchy as a residence for the Duke in Wales. In 2013, the Duchy's office in Cornwall moved from Liskeard to Restormel Manor's old farm buildings. In 2014, the Duchy purchased the southern half of the Port Eliot estate from Lord St Germans. The Duchy owns The Oval cricket ground in London and so the Duchy has very substantial landholdings across the country.

The Duchy Council, called the Prince's Council, meets twice a year and is chaired by the Duke. The Prince's Council is a non-executive body which provides advice to the Duke with regard to the management of the Duchy.

The Cornish use the Loyal Toast "The King and The Duke of Cornwall", rather than simply "The King".

Elsewhere, in the British Isles there are similar unique circumstances. In the county palatine of Lancashire, which includes Lancashire, Merseyside, Greater Manchester and Furness area of Cumbria, Lancastrians use the Loyal Toast "The King, Duke of Lancaster", rather than simply "The King". In the Channel Islands, the British monarch is known informally as the Duke of Normandy. The Channel Islands are the last remaining part of the former Duchy of Normandy to remain under the rule of the British monarch. Islanders use the Loyal Toast "The Duke of Normandy, our King", or "The King, our Duke" rather than simply "The King" as used in the UK. In the Isle of Man, the British monarch is known as the Lord of Mann as the Lord Proprietor and Head of State of the Isle of Man, but before 1504 the title was King of Mann. So Islanders from the Isle of Man use the Loyal Toast "The King, Lord of Mann" rather than simply "The King" as used in the UK.

The Duchy of Cornwall is one of two royal duchies that remain in the UK: the other is the Duchy of Lancaster which provides income to the Duke of Lancaster, a title which is held by the British monarch.

https://duchyofcornwall.org/
https://poundbury.co.uk/
https://www.highgrovegardens.com/

FUN FACT: DID YOU KNOW THAT…..

Cornwall famously has an ongoing rivalry with the neighbouring county of Devon about how best to do a cream tea which consists of a cup of tea and a scone with clotted cream and jam. The heart of the lengthy and fierce debate rests around what is the correct order to put the layers of clotted cream and jam on the scone! Cornwall says that it is the jam first and then the clotted cream! While Devon says that it is the clotted cream first and then the jam! But do take time to enjoy a classic Cornish cream tea or Devonshire cream tea as either option shouldn't be missed!

FORMER RAILWAY OWNED HOTELS:

The railway companies used to own hotels across their networks to encourage travellers to use the railways for business and leisure and encourage tourism. Some were city centre hotels; others were resort hotels or located at ferry and ocean liner ports. Some survived to become part of British Transport Hotels in 1962. Eventually this was privatised in 1983.

The surviving former railway owned hotels in the Great Western area include:

- Great Western Royal Hotel (GWR London Paddington) now Hilton London Paddington
- Great Western Hotel (GWR Reading) now the Malmaison Reading
- Great Western Hotel (GWR Taunton)
- Fishguard Bay Hotel (GWR Fishguard Harbour)
- Great Western Hotel (GWR Torquay) now Grand Hotel Torquay
- Manor House Hotel (GWR Moretonhampstead) now Bovey Castle Hotel
- Duke of Cornwall Hotel (GWR Plymouth Millbay Docks)
- Great Western Hotel (GWR Newquay)
- Fowey Hotel (GWR Fowey) now Harbour Hotel Fowey
- Falmouth Hotel (GWR Falmouth)
- Tregenna Castle Hotel (GWR St Ives)
- Queens Hotel (GWR Penzance)
- Metropole Hotel (SR Padstow) now Harbour Hotel Padstow

Great Western Royal Hotel, London Paddington
(now Hilton London Paddington)
(c) National Railway Museum / Science Museum

Tregenna Castle Hotel, St Ives
(c) National Railway Museum / Science Museum Group

Falmouth Hotel, Falmouth (c) Author's Collection

Metropole Hotel, Padstow (now Harbour Hotel Padstow) (c) Author's Collection

Manor House Hotel, Moretonhampstead (now Bovey Castle Hotel)
(c) National Railway Museum / Science Museum Group

Fishguard Bay Hotel, Fishguard Harbour
(c) National Railway Museum / Science Museum Group

Great Western Hotel, Torquay (now Grand Hotel Torquay) (c) Author's Collection

Duke of Cornwall Hotel, Plymouth Millbay Docks (c) Author's Collection

Route Description

Route Description

London Paddington is one of London's grandest and most elegant stations and is an important monument to the work of Isambard Kingdom Brunel. It was built by the Great Western Railway in 1854 and was designed by the legendary engineer Isambard Kingdom Brunel. This famous engineer also designed the S.S. Great Britain, the Clifton Suspension Bridge and the Royal Albert Bridge at Saltash. London Paddington is famous for its association with *Paddington Bear* and there is a statue of him on Platform 1. There is also the *Paddington Bear Shop* on and *Paddington Bear Café* on the Lawn. Between Platforms 8 and 9 there is a statue of Isambard Kingdom Brunel. On Armistice Day 1922, a memorial to the employees of the GWR who died during the First World War was unveiled by Viscount Churchill. The bronze memorial, depicting a soldier reading a letter, was sculpted by Charles Sargeant Jagger and stands on platform 1. London Paddington is home to the *Great Western Railway Paddington Band*, the last railway band in England. It plays on Friday evenings on the main concourse. The concourse of the station is called "The Lawn". The former goods depot can be seen on the right as trains leave the station. This is now redeveloped as Paddington Waterside and links the station with the canalside of the *Grand Union Canal*.

In its heyday and even today, London Paddington was the "Gateway to the West" and the starting point for journeys to the Thames Valley, West Country, the Cotswolds and South Wales. The station is fronted by the magnificent former Great Western Royal Hotel, which remains a prestigious hotel known as the *Hilton London Paddington*. In its heyday London Paddington was the starting point for such famous expresses as the Cornish Riviera Express, the Royal Duchy, the Torbay Express, the Bristolian, the Red Dragon, the Pembroke Coast Express, the Cathedrals Express, the Inter-City and the Cambrian Coast Express. From 1998 London Paddington also became the gateway to the world's busiest airport when it became the terminus of the *Heathrow Express* service to London Heathrow Airport. Today London Paddington is operated by Network Rail as one of its 20 *Major Stations*.

HEATHROW EXPRESS:

The Heathrow Express is one of London's four Airport Express services along with the Gatwick Express, Stansted Express and Luton Airport Express.

It was launched in 1998 with the opening of the new rail link between London Paddington and London Heathrow Airport. The express service is operated by Heathrow Airport in partnership with Great Western Railway and takes 15 minutes. At London Paddington the services tend to use the dedicated Platforms 6 and 7. There are two stops at Heathrow: Heathrow Central, serving Terminals 2 and 3 and Heathrow Terminal 5. Until the opening of Terminal 5 on 27 March 2008, the Heathrow Express terminated at Heathrow Terminal 4. In 2010, Heathrow Express introduced a dedicated shuttle between Heathrow Central and Terminal 4.

Website: www.heathrowexpress.com

TFL ELIZABETH LINE:

The Elizabeth line stretches more than 100km from Reading and Heathrow in the west through central tunnels across to Shenfield and Abbey Wood in the east.

Detailed plans for what became the Elizabeth line started in earnest in 2001. Under an agreement between Transport for London (TfL) and the Department for Transport, the project organisation Crossrail Limited was created as a subsidiary of TfL in December 2008.

In February 2016 Queen Elizabeth II unveiled the new roundel for the Elizabeth line. A new moquette seating pattern was designed by Wallace Sewell for use on the line. The purple colour of the line and logo is reflected in the pattern.

Train services on the Elizabeth Line launched in various phases until the full line opened in 2022. TfL Rail services opened between London Liverpool Street and Shenfield May 2015 to form what would become the eastern branch of the Elizabeth line. In 2018 services to the west of London begin running as TfL Rail between London Paddington and Heathrow Airport, replacing the existing Heathrow Connect service and part of the Great Western inner suburban service. In 2019 services started between London Paddington and Reading. Finally Queen Elizabeth II formally opened the line on 18 May 2022. Elizabeth line services started on Tuesday 24 May 2022, with 10 stations under central London.

The Elizabeth line is London's first accessible railway. It is the result of the biggest infrastructure project in a generation and, as a concept, can trace its history back over a century. The Elizabeth line runs through London's first new deep tube tunnels in the 21st century. The new line connects the mainline stations at London Paddington and London Liverpool Street with Heathrow Airport and Reading in the west, and with Shenfield and Abbey Wood in the east. It increases central London's rail capacity by 10%, taking pressure off some of London Underground's busiest interchanges. The Elizabeth line is unique on the London Underground in that surface stock trains (Aventra trains built by Bombardier in Derby) run in tube tunnels under the Capital, and far out into Berkshire and Essex on the surface.

A new depot at Old Oak Common houses and maintains 42 of the Elizabeth line's 70 new trains at a time and includes many novel features. The building incorporates heating and cooling from ground sources, with solar panels and rainwater harvesting to wash trains. An automatic system scans trains as they enter, reducing the overall time needed for maintenance.

Website: https://tfl.gov.uk/modes/elizabeth-line/

Throughout this "Through the Window" guide we describe views as being left or right from the train facing in the direction of travel out of London.

London Paddington to Reading:

On leaving **London Paddington**, the train follows the elevated M40 motorway seen on the right briefly before emerging into an area of high rise development. **Royal Oak** station and **Westbourne Park** station are passed within a few minutes of departure from Paddington. Kensal Green cemetery and Old Oak Common train depot are passed to the right, while to the left can be seen the pinnacles of Wormwood Scrubs. Kensal Green cemetery is where Thackeray, Leigh Hunt, Isambard Kingdom Brunel and other famous people are buried. Wormwood Scrubs is the big prison. The prison was originally built by convict labour and houses 1400 prisoners. During the First World War, however, Wormwood Scrubs was an important airfield for the RAF.

To the left as you pass the Old Oak Common train depot can be seen North Pole Depot which was built for the maintenance of the Eurostar trains through the Channel Tunnel. This area is also the proposed location for the new **Old Oak Common** station which will be a new transport superhub in West London linking the Great Western Main Line to the new HS2 high speed line between

London Euston and Birmingham Curzon Street (due to open in the early 2030s) offering quick, reliable, and comfortable journeys to the Midlands, the North and Scotland.

The former industrial area around Old Oak and Park Royal is set to be one of the largest regeneration sites in the UK. Plans to transform the wider area around the station are led by the Mayor of London's Old Oak and Park Royal Development Corporation (OPDC). Over 100 acres has been marked for development and there are plans to create 25,000 new homes and 56,000 new jobs in the area.

Next **Acton Main Line** station is passed through. London Underground trains share the route for much of the way to **Ealing Broadway** and then the surroundings become more suburban.

Beyond **West Ealing**, the Greenford branch diverges off to the right via a triangular junction and Hanwell Recreation Ground can be seen on the right, and beyond **Hanwell & Elthorne** station the tower of Hanwell Church can be seen on the right. In its churchyard lies Jonas Hanway, the man who introduced the umbrella to Britain in 1750. Soon the line is carried high over the River Brent on the 8 arched Warncliffe Viaduct built in 1837. Soon **Southall** is reached and to the left can be seen the Southall Locomotive Depot which is now used as the London base for [West Coast Railways](#) and Jeremy Hosking's [Locomotive Services TOC Ltd](#). Just beyond Southall the line crosses the [Grand Junction Canal](#) and soon **Hayes & Harlington** is reached. After **West Drayton** station the River Colne is crossed. Shortly after this the line to Heathrow Airport can be seen diverging from the mainline via a flyover to the left. Then **Iver** station is reached. The [Grand Junction Canal](#) soon draws up close to the line on the right just as **Langley** station is reached.

The French style, domed station at **Slough** dates from 1838 in parts. Here the branch line to Windsor & Eton Central can be seen branching off to the left soon after the station. Before this branch line was opened in 1850 Queen Victoria used Slough station when she travelled to Windsor Castle. The River Thames divides Windsor from its close but no less famous neighbour Eton. After leaving Slough a number of interesting factories line the route, notably the impressive brick former home of [Horlicks](#) to the right at the iconic Horlicks Factory. This was built in 1908 and finally closed in 2018. The iconic [Horlicks Factory](#) is now being regenerated as apartments by Berkeley Group.

FUN FACT: DID YOU KNOW THAT…..

Slough Trading Estate, founded in 1925, is the largest industrial estate in single private ownership in Europe with over 17,000 jobs in 400 businesses.

After Slough the landscape becomes more rural, while to the left can be seen the continuous stream of planes on their final approach to London Heathrow airport. Soon **Burnham** station is passed and then **Taplow**. To the right is Taplow's 1912 church with its distinctive green spire, and then the train makes its first crossing of the River Thames. Maidenhead Bridge with its two graceful shallow brick arches spanning the river is one of Brunel's masterpieces. Opened in 1837, it confounded its critics, who firmly believed that such flat arches would surely collapse. The bridge also features in J.M.W. Turner's famous painting, *Rain, Steam and Speed*. Maidenhead still retains echoes of its Edwardian charm by the river.

Maidenhead station is where the [Bourne End and Marlow Branch](#) (often nicknamed as the Marlow Donkey) can be seen branching off to the right.

To the right of the line after **Twyford** station, where the Regatta Line branch to Henley on Thames can be seen joining the mainline on the right, are the lakes and flooded gravel pits that surround the River Loddon, a River Thames tributary. A deep cutting, the Sonning Cutting, south of Sonning then takes the line towards Reading. The railway enters the town with the River Thames right next to the line on the right hand side. To the right can be seen the white façade of [Caversham Park](#), a 1850s mansion that housed [BBC Monitoring](#) from 1943 to 2018. In 2018 it was sold by the BBC to [Beechcroft Developments](#) and converted into retirement village. Before it arrives at Reading station, the line crosses the River Kennet, the River Thames' link with the Kennet & Avon Canal and the recently reopened waterway route to Bath and Bristol. On the left the great gas holders are passed. Also the line from London Waterloo can be seen on the left as the train enters **Reading** station.

Reading is a thriving university town and shopping and business centre. Reading still has a good variety of 19th century architecture, notably the Royal Berkshire Hospital of 1837 and the 1870s municipal buildings by Waterhouse. The ruins of the Cluniac abbey, founded by King Henry I in the 12th century, underline the town's historic importance. Reading dates from the 8th century. It was an important trading and ecclesiastical centre in the Middle Ages, the site of [Reading Abbey](#), one of the largest and richest monasteries of medieval England with strong royal connections, of which the 12th-century abbey gateway and significant ancient ruins remain. [Reading Museum](#) tells the story of the town.

Reading station is an important junction with lines running to Oxford and the Midlands, the West Country and the South West via Basingstoke. Another line to London Waterloo also connects with routes to Surrey and Kent. Reading station has a gracious Italianate façade of 1870, crowned with a decorative clock tower, but however to the side is the new station complete with shopping arcade. Today Reading is operated by Network Rail as one of its 20 [Major Stations](#). Outside Reading railway station is the former Great Western Hotel which is now the [Malmaison Reading.](#) From Reading there are regular [RailAir](#) express coach services to London Heathrow Airport.

> **FUN FACT: DID YOU KNOW THAT…..**
>
> The first restaurant of the iconic "Little Chef" restaurant chain opened in Reading in 1958. The brand was inspired by American style roadside diners. The restaurant chain was famous for the "Olympic Breakfast" – its version of a full English Breakfast – as well as its "Early Starter" and "Jubilee Pancakes". There were 12 restaurants located around England by 1965. The chain expanded rapidly throughout the 1970s, and its parent company would acquire the Happy Eater chain in the 1980s, its only major roadside competitor. When its owners converted all Happy Eater restaurants to Little Chef in the late 1990s, this allowed it to peak in scale with 439 restaurants. Sadly in the 2000s the brand started a dramatic decline and was closed in 2018.

> **FUN FACT: DID YOU KNOW THAT…..**
>
> Reading University was founded in 1892 as University College, Reading, a University of Oxford extension college by the University of Oxford's Christ Church College. It only gained independence from University of Oxford and received the power to grant its own degrees in 1926 by royal charter from King George V and was the only university to receive such a charter between the two world wars.
>
> Website: https://www.reading.ac.uk/

Reading to Taunton:

On leaving **Reading** the line to the West Country leaves the mainline to Bristol, Oxford and the Midlands which can be seen heading off to the right. To the right are the fields alongside the River Thames that every year around the August Bank Holiday weekend are host to the *Reading Festival* which is one of the UK's major summer music festivals and was launched in 1971.

The train then runs past housing estates to **Reading West**, and then soon enters open country as they cross the River Kennet. The line to Basingstoke is soon seen diverging off to the left. From this point the river and the Kennet & Avon Canal are never far from the line, and the canal with its restored locks, its handsome brick bridges and its brightly painted narrow boats is an enjoyable feature of the journey. With the gravel works and lakes of the Kennet valley to the left, the line passes under the M4 and then **Theale** comes into view, marked by its large early Victorian church. The next station is **Aldermaston**, but its village with its pretty brick cottages is over a mile to the south of the station. Since 1950 it is also home to the UK Government's *Atomic Weapons Establishment (AWE)* and has become synonymous with CND (Campaign for Nuclear Disarmament) protest marches ever since. In a historic first, Britain's first roadside petrol filling station was opened by The AA on the Bath Road near Aldermaston on 2 March 1919. Closer to hand is Midgham Church, Victorian and decorative, and attractively placed in a field just to the west of **Midgham** station. At Thatcham, another station some distance from its town, there is a canal lock just to the left.

Approaching Newbury, the train passes *Newbury Racecourse* to the left, whose weather boarded station, **Newbury Racecourse**, still retains its GWR name boards. At **Newbury** station, little of the town can be seen, but the centre is not far away, easily accessible on foot.

Newbury has plenty to offer the visitor. The great 16th century church and 17th century cloth hall, which now houses a museum, reveal the town's former wealth as a centre of the wool trade. In the 15th century over 1000 wool weavers were employed here, in what was England's first true factory. Prosperity continued in later centuries, particularly after the opening of the *Kennet & Avon Canal*, which winds its way through the town centre, and the legacy is an interesting variety of buildings from all periods, including some groups of almshouses and a Victorian corn exchange. Newbury is also famous for the two Civil War battles that were fought near the town.

Leaving Newbury, the train enters a wooded stretch, with glimpses of the pretty village of Hamstead Marshall to the left as it passes the close group of the mill, the pub and the canal lock. To the right is the classical façade of 18th century Benham House, set in its Capability Brown park. **Kintbury** village is to the south of its station, clustered around its large church. After Kintbury the river valley becomes more defined and the line runs along the southern slopes with good views across to the northern side, beyond the river and the canal. **Hungerford** is a handsome town, with all its main buildings in one street which climbs southwards away from the river. From the railway bridge just west of the station, there is a clear view of the town centre to the left, with its good range of 18th and 19th century buildings, but trains approaching from the west offer the best view of the church and its vicarage, pleasantly set beside the river and the canal. West of Hungerford the line overlooks the canal and the river valley, and then it crosses the canal again near Froxfield, where the decorative gothic façade of the almshouses founded by the Duchess of Somerset in 1694 can be clearly seen.

Railway and canal now run close together to Little Bedwyn, a delightful little village with its 12th century church, its row of 1860s estate cottages, all in coloured brick, and the 18th century buildings by the canal and lock. Locks appear quite frequently now as the canal climbs towards its summit, a few miles to the south west, and the train soon reaches **Bedwyn**. Near the station is Great Bedwyn's large church with its grand central tower and pretty graveyard, and a short walk away is the attractive village.

After Bedwyn the line continues west through the rolling countryside of the Marlborough Downs. The *Kennet & Avon Canal* continues to parallel the railway to the left and the famous *Crofton Beam Engines* at Crofton Pumping Station are passed to the right and then the canal disappears into a tunnel near Savernake.

FUN FACT: DID YOU KNOW THAT…..

Crofton Pumping Station on the Kennet and Avon Canal in Wiltshire houses two working beam engines that are historic engineering masterpieces and are among the oldest beam engines in the world. The Boulton and Watt engine, built in 1812, is the oldest beam engine in the world still in its original setting and carrying out its original job. The Harvey & Co. of Hayle, Cornwall engine, built in 1846 and modified in 1905, is one of the few remaining operating engines of its type.

It is a rare survivor of the technology which enabled British engineers to drain mines and supply towns and cities with water throughout the world. It is one of the most significant industrial heritage sites in the United Kingdom and a fascinating visitor attraction that enables the visitor to step into our industrial and social history and turn back the clock to a time when steam was king.

Website: https://www.croftonbeamengines.org/

Soon the village of Woolton Rivers can be seen to the right as the line draws alongside Martinsell Hill. The summit of which is crowned by a large prehistoric camp covering more than 30 acres. The hill rises 947 ft high and commands fine views across Salisbury Plain which stretches away to the left of the railway line.

Soon the line reaches **Pewsey** station with its village to the left, with its church rising above the village. Salisbury Plain continues to stretch away to the left. To the right can be seen Picked Hill and Woodborough Hill. Due north from here lies the ancient site of [Avebury](#) one of the many ancient sites that lie alongside this route to the west. To the right also can be seen Milk Hill and its famous [Pewsey White Horse](#). This horse only dates from 1812 but some of the other white horses in this part of the country are very ancient including the Westbury White Horse which the line passes later on in the journey. Then to the right can be seen the village of Woodborough. The ancient earthwork of Rybury Camp can be seen to the right. While to the left is the village of Beechingstoke and the vast expanse of Salisbury Plain stretching away to the south. Then a broad valley opens up to the right and the line bends south west. The village of Potterne can be seen to the right, and on the left the village of Great Cheverell appears. Also to the left the long line of Salisbury Plain forms the horizon. Coulston Hill and Stoke Hill are seen as a background to the village of East Coulston while a little further on Edington Hill can be seen behind the village of Edington. This village has the beautiful Priory Church at its heart. This splendid piece of 14th century architecture was built by William de Edyndune, who became Bishop of Winchester and began the important rebuilding of Winchester Cathedral which was completed by his successor William of Wykeham.

The next hill viewed to the left is Westbury Hill and at the summit can be seen the great earthwork of [Bratton Camp](#) with fine trenches clearly marked by the long ridges on the hillside. Legend tells that it was at this spot that the Danish King Guthrum retired after suffering a heavy defeat by King Alfred the Great at the Battle of Ethandune in 878.

Westbury Hill juts out prominently from the main form of Salisbury Plain at this point and soon another famous landmark comes into view on its western slopes. This is the famous [Westbury White Horse](#). Unlike its counterpart we saw earlier in the journey at Milk Hill near Pewsey, this White Horse is very ancient. Legend tells how it may have been cut to commemorate King Alfred the Great's great victory over King Guthrum. But having become overgrown in places it was recut in 1778 and received further attention in 1873. It measures 175 ft from head to tail and stands 107 ft high.

Soon the Westbury avoiding line can be seen diverging off to the left and if the train is not stopping at Westbury then it will take the avoiding line and the town can be seen to the left. However if the train is calling at Westbury station then it will continue and the line from Bristol can be seen joining the mainline from the right. Then the train enters **Westbury** station. This station is an important junction for trains to Bristol and Salisbury.

After leaving Westbury the line to Salisbury can be seen diverging to the left and soon the Westbury avoiding line rejoins the mainline from the left. Away to the left can be seen Cley Hill rising in the distance. Like many high hills in this part of England it too has a prehistoric camp at the summit. The hill rises to 800 ft and commands fine views. Historically it is of interest as it was one of the sites chosen for the great beacon fires that gave warning of the approach of the Spanish Armada. Soon the valley of the Frome is reached. Again Frome station, like Westbury, has an avoiding line to allow express trains to bypass the station. This is soon seen diverging off to the left. Just before entering **Frome** station the disused line to Radstock can be seen joining the mainline from the right. After leaving Frome the avoiding line rejoins from the left and the journey continues westwards.

Cley Hill continues to keep the line company after Frome and the hill could be considered as the western outpost of Salisbury Plain as soon we enter a different landscape. The change is marked almost at once by the fine mass of woodland around [Longleat House](#), the ancestral home of the Most Hon. The Marquess of Bath. The house stands beside a beautiful lake in a widespread deer park, hidden from view by the beautiful Longleat Woods to the left.

LONGLEAT HOUSE:

Longleat House is widely regarded as one of the finest examples of Elizabethan architecture in Britain. It is the ancestral home of the Marquesses of Bath. In 1949 Longleat House became the first stately home in Britain to be opened to the public on a commercial basis. Longleat Safari Park opened in 1966 as the first drive-through safari park outside Africa, and is home to over 500 animals, including giraffe, monkeys, rhino, lion, tigers and wolves. Today you can see their amazing animals by car, foot, train, bus and boat. The 9,800-acre estate, of which the park occupies 900 acres, has long been one of the top British tourist attractions, and has motivated other large landowners to generate income from their heritage too.

Website: https://www.longleat.co.uk/

To the right spreads Postlebury Wood over Postlebury hill. These woodlands form part of Witham Park. Soon the village of Witham Friary is passed. Here the line to the Cranmore and now home of the *East Somerset Railway* diverges from the mainline to the right. Soon the village of Upton Noble lies to the right.

EAST SOMERSET RAILWAY:

The East Somerset Railway is a heritage steam railway that operates between Cranmore and Mendip Vale through the beautiful Mendip countryside. It has a mainline connection but this section is used by freight trains to the Merehead Quarry. The heritage railway was founded by David Shepherd, the famous wildlife artist and conservationist, in 1971. At Cranmore station you can explore the David Shepherd Discovery Centre which celebrates the history of the railway and the life of the world famous wildlife artist whose vision for the railway made it what it is today.

Website: https://eastsomersetrailway.com/

The little River Brue now flows beside the line on the left, and soon the little town of **Bruton** is reached. On the right the land slopes down gently into the valley of the Brue and its tributary, the River Alham, we have a view of the distant Mendip Hills. Soon the ancient town of Castle Cary lies to the left and **Castle Cary** station is reached. This is close to where the *Glastonbury Festival* is held at Worthy Farm and is one of the world's most legendary music festivals. Just after the station the line to Yeovil, Dorchester and Weymouth diverges left from the mainline.

GLASTONBURY FESTIVAL:

The Glastonbury Festival is the UK's greatest music festival and was founded by Michael Eavis in 1970 and is held most years at Worthy Farm. It is the largest green space open air music and performing arts festival in the world and a template for all the festivals that have come after it. The festival takes place in a beautiful location – 900 acres in the Vale of Avalon, an area steeped in symbolism, mythology and religious traditions dating back many hundreds of years overlooked by Glastonbury Tor and with stunning views across the Somerset Levels. Over the decades it has gained an iconic and legendary status in the event calendar and is attended by around 175,000 people and is broadcast on TV too. In 2014, the V&A Museum acquired guardianship of the Glastonbury Festival Archive, an eclectic and growing resource that reveals how the Festival has developed over the past 50 years to become the global cultural phenomenon that it is today. It is famed for the iconic Pyramid Stage and sells out in minutes, and has hosted many of music's most important and high-profile performers since its inception in 1970.

Website: https://www.glastonburyfestivals.co.uk/

A striking landmark that can be seen to the right, looking west, is Glastonbury Tor, a prominent hill with the ruined chapel of St Michael on its summit. Soon on the left can be seen the church tower of Lovington. While also on the left in the distance can be seen *Cadbury Castle*. Around the steep sides of the hill are four lines of earthworks and this camp is said to have been the last British stronghold in the West to hold out against the Romans. Wheathill Church stands close to the line on the left, and East Lydford Church on the right, with Glastonbury Tor still visible in the distance.

Next is the village of Keinton Mandeville on the right. This village is the birthplace of Sir Henry Irving in 1838. He was a famous actor in the Victorian era and inspiration for Dracula. Pennard Hill near Glastonbury rises up 400 ft on the right. While on the left is the village of Charlton Adam and its church tower. Then Charlton Mackrell is passed on the right. To the right appears Dundon Hill beyond Copley Wood. Soon we reach Somerton. It is a picturesque little place with an ancient market cross and other old buildings. It stands of the River Cary. After passing Somerton the railway enters Somerton Tunnel, and it is the first tunnel after leaving London. After the tunnel the small market town of Langport is passed. This town lies on the River Parrett. Hills rise either side of the railway here, but the valley of the Parrett broadens out into another expanse of low lying country. The stretch lying immediately to the right is Aller Moor and where the hills subside into the valley is the village of Aller. This is where King Alfred the Great is said to have baptised King Guthrun and many of his followers in the Saxon font which can still be seen in Aller Church soon after the battle of Ethandune. Away to the right beyond the villages of Othery and Middlezoy stretches Sedgemoor, famous for the site of the battle of Sedgemoor which ended the Duke of Monmouth's rebellion in 1685.

The Polden Hills can be seen rising beyond the level stretch of Sedgemoor, while to the left on the higher ground bordering West Sedge Moor is seen the Parkfield Monument, erected in 1768 by the Earl of Chatham to commemorate Sir William Pynsent. Also on the left is the village of Stoke St Gregory. To the right can be seen the great Burrow Bridge Mound, identified by legend as 'King Alfred's Fort', and actually used as a fort during the Civil Wars. Athelney is close to the junction of the River Tone and River Parrett. Soon the line passes the Isle of Athelney to the left and the legendary location of the humble cottage where King Alfred the Great had his telling off after burning the cakes! Here in these marshes he took refuge and rested while preparing the final assault against the Danes. The Isle is a slight rise above the level of the flat lands; and in medieval times there was an abbey, but now there is a pillar erected in 1801, with an inscription commemorating King Alfred the Great. Looking ahead to the right a distant view can be seen of the Quantock Hills. A little way beyond the Isle of Athelney to the right can be seen the village of Lyng. While on the left beyond the level stretch of Curry Moor, through which flows the River Tone, is seen the village of North Curry. In the distance are the Blackdown Hills.

Soon the line joins the mainline from Bristol to Taunton via a flyover and the [Bridgewater & Taunton Canal](#) can be seen on the right. While on the left the River Tone follows the line past the village of Creech St Michael whose church is famous for the extremely ancient carving of the Holy Trinity above the west door. The neighbouring village of Ruishton also presents an ancient church with a fine tower. The M5 soon crosses the railway and then **Taunton** station is reached.

Taunton is a fine town with a rich history. [Taunton Castle](#) (now home to the Museum of Somerset and the [Castle Hotel](#)) was founded in the 8th century by King Ina, King of the West Saxons, and a large part of the medieval building still remains. Taunton also played an important role in the English Civil War and was chosen by the Duke of Monmouth as the place where he proclaimed himself King. An event which had its sequel in the Bloody Assize held here by Judge Jeffreys. Outside Taunton railway station is the [Great Western Hotel](#).

FUN FACT: DID YOU KNOW THAT…..

Taunton in Somerset was the first town in the UK to be lit permanently by electric street lighting in 1881. This was 12 months before the Electric Lighting Act of 1882 which enforced the switch from oil lamps to electric across the UK.

FUN FACT: DID YOU KNOW THAT…..

The West Country including Somerset (along with Devon, Herefordshire, Gloucestershire and Worcestershire) is famed for its orchards and is a major cider producing area. There are more than 400 different varieties of cider apple grown in Somerset alone, which is enough to keep the keenest scrumper busy. Indeed, England consumes more cider per capita than any other country in the world and is the largest producer of cider in Europe.

FUN FACT: DID YOU KNOW THAT…..

Ten pin bowling has its origins in the game of Somerset skittles, that was played on outside lawns with nine wooden pins. Today ten pin bowling is mainly played in indoor bowling alleys and remains a popular game.

FUN FACT: DID YOU KNOW THAT…..

The 'Frome Hoard' is the largest collection of Roman coins ever found in a single container and can now be seen in the Museum of Somerset at Taunton.

Taunton to Exeter St Davids:

Soon after leaving Taunton a view across to the Blackdown Hills opens out to the left and the Wellington obelisk is seen on the ridge. On the right is seen [Taunton School](), a notable public school, located at Staplegrove. The school opened its history in 1847 as the Independent College, a centre of education for boys from nonconformist families. The buildings date from 1870.

The ancient octagonal church tower on the left is that of Bishop's Hull. To the right is the village of Norton Fitzwarren and site of **Norton Fitzwarren** station is soon reached. This station was where the branches to Barnstaple and Minehead diverged off to the right. Sadly only the Minehead line now remains and is home to the [West Somerset Railway](). On the left the village of Bradford on Tone appears.

WEST SOMERSET RAILWAY:

The West Somerset Railway is a heritage steam railway that offers 20 miles of heritage railway through stunning Somerset countryside and coast. It operates regular services between Minehead and Bishop's Lydeard, near Taunton. It is the longest independent railway in Britain. The line meanders through the Quantock Hills, an area of outstanding natural beauty and along the Bristol Channel Coast. . It has a mainline connection which is used by occasional through excursion trains.

Website: https://www.west-somerset-railway.co.uk/

The Blackdown Hills and the [Wellington Monument]() come into closer view as we head south west. Then the town of Wellington is passed. There are two Wellingtons – one in Somerset and one in Shropshire. However it is this Somerset Wellington that gives the great Iron Duke and the Duke of Wellington their title. Again to the left can be seen the Wellington Monument erected in honour of the Battle of Waterloo and the Duke of Wellington's victory. Wellington is also home to the notable public school, [Wellington School](). Soon the village of Sampford Arundel is passed to the left and Culmstock Beacon can be seen on the western end of the Blackdown Hills. After this the landscape slopes down into the Culm Valley.

FUN FACT: DID YOU KNOW THAT…..

It was while descending Wellington Bank in Somerset in 1904 with an Ocean Mails boat train from Plymouth to London Paddington that GWR No 3440 City of Truro steam locomotive found its place in history and broke a speed record. On 9th May 1904 City of Truro achieved a speed of 102.3mph on the descent of Wellington Bank between Exeter and Taunton. It was not only the first locomotive to reach and pass the magical speed of 100mph, but the first vehicle of any kind to reach such a milestone. This gave it iconic and legendary status and as a result it is now preserved as part of the National Railway Museum collection and is on static display at the STEAM Museum of the Great Western Railway in Swindon.

FUN FACT: DID YOU KNOW THAT…..

The countryside around Tiverton is famed for its dairy farming and in the 1920s and 30s it was here that the concept of Young Farmers Clubs was founded starting with the Culm Valley Young Farmers Club and the national network that is the National Federation of Young Farmers Clubs. Today it is one of the largest rural youth organisations in the UK and is dedicated to young people who have a love for agriculture and rural life.

Website: https://www.nfyfc.org.uk

At this point the train has started the ascent of Wellington Bank which is a steep gradient and soon enters Whiteball Tunnel. Soon the village of Burlescombe is seen on the left and behind it is the M5 motorway which soon runs alongside the railway. To the right is the Grand Western Canal. This connects the River Tone with the River Exe which the canal enters at Tiverton. Soon the village of Sampford Peverel is seen to the right and **Tiverton Parkway** station is reached alongside the M5 motorway.

After leaving Tiverton Parkway to the north west on the right of the line can be seen Barton Hill. To the left across the Culm Valley is the village of Kentisbeare. Soon the village of Willand is passed. The Culm River is an important tributary of the River Exe, coming down from the southern slopes of the Blackdown Hills. Soon the next settlement passed is Cullompton. All the way the M5 parallels the railway line to the left. The railway then crosses the River Culm and to the right appears the village of Bradninch. Bradninch was a chartered borough as long ago as 1208 and from the time of King Edward II to that of King Henry VII returned two Members of Parliament. Bradninch Manor House which stands to the right on the outskirts of the village, is one of the finest examples of an Elizabethan interior in the country. Some of the rooms are finely carved and panelled. King Charles I stayed at the old Rectory during the Civil War.

The wooded hill which rises prominently close to the railway on the left is Dolbury Hill. Rising sharply out of the landscape by Killerton Park it checks the River Culm on its course and forces it to make a wide detour. The M5 motorway also disappears from view behind the hill. Soon the River Culm can be seen again on the left and from the right it is joined by the River Exe. The village of Rewe is passed by close to the railway on the left. Then again on the left the village of Stoke Canon is passed. Then across the River Exe can be seen the village of Brampford Speke. Just after Stoke Canon the River Exe passes under the railway to join the River Culm with the beautiful Stoke Woods rising up to the right.

The River Exe is a beautiful and interesting river, beginning its story way up in the hills and rocky tors of Exmoor. It rises in the centre of Exmoor Forest only a few miles from the North Devon coast but heads across Devon to find its way into the sea on the South Devon coast at Exmouth. At Tiverton it receives the River Lowman, made famous by Blackmore in the 'Lorna Doone'.

Soon the railway heads down into the historic city of Exeter. At Cowley Bridge the *Tarka Valley Line* (one of the *Great Scenic Railways of Devon & Cornwall*) from Barnstaple can be seen joining the mainline from the right. The *Dartmoor Line* (one of the *Great Scenic Railways of Devon & Cornwall*) from Okehampton also joins. As we approach Exeter the city spreads itself out on the hill to the left and soon **Exeter St Davids** station is reached.

> **FUN FACT: DID YOU KNOW THAT…..**
>
> In 1934 Sir Allen Lane famously got inspiration for creation of *Penguin Books* while waiting for a train at Exeter St Davids. Penguin Books famously transformed publishing industry with its affordable paperbacks that brought books to the masses. In April 2023 a Penguin Books vending machine was installed at Exeter St Davids rail station in the main entrance hall by a partnership of Penguin Books, Exeter UNESCO City of Literature and Great Western Railway. This book vending machine will allow passengers to buy a wide range of Penguin Books.

Exeter was a fortified town and a busy port from the Roman period onwards, but it was the Normans who developed the city as it stands today. Their legacy is the great *Exeter Cathedral* with its flanking Norman towers. Greatly expanded during the Middle Ages, the cathedral is also known for its vaulting and 14th century sculptures in the west front. It was the River Exe and the port that made Exeter a wealthy city in the Middle Ages and the surviving timber framed buildings reflect this. In order to maintain its wealth, the city built its ship canal to the sea, from 1564. Exeter today is a thriving city with an exciting past. Indeed Exeter is one of the oldest cities in the West Country as always been a capital in a wider sense than being the county town of Devon. Its position here in the West Country is similar to that of Winchester to the ancient kingdom of Wessex. Exeter is also a bustling commercial city and a great railway centre. At Exeter there is the *Dartmoor Explorer* bus service to Plymouth via Moretonhampstead, Princetown and Yelverton across Dartmoor. There are regular bus services from Exeter St Davids to Exeter Airport.

Here at Exeter St Davids the former Southern Railway line from London Waterloo joins the Great Western mainline. In its heyday Southern Railway expresses from Waterloo crossed with Great Western ones from Paddington each heading in opposite directions. Southern ones going north via Okehampton and down into Plymouth via Tavistock, while Great Western ones went south via the famous sea wall section at Dawlish to Plymouth. Sadly today only the Great Western route survives as a through mainline.

Exeter St Davids to Plymouth:

Shortly after leaving **Exeter St Davids** station the line to London Waterloo diverges from the mainline to the left and heads up the steep Exeter Incline to Exeter Central station. The line from Exeter St Davids and Exeter Central east towards London Waterloo is known as the *East Devon Line* as far as Axminster (one of the *Great Scenic Railways of Devon & Cornwall*). There is also the *Avocet Line* to Exmouth (one of the *Great Scenic Railways of Devon & Cornwall*).

As our train leaves Exeter and heads westwards we pass **Exeter St Thomas** station and a view of the magnificent *Exeter Cathedral* and the city opens up to the left. We then pass the new rail station at **Marsh Barton** that opened on 4 July 2023. This station serves Exeter's largest industrial estate and is in close proximity to the Riverside Valley Park which offers wonderful routes for walking and cycling alongside the River Exe. It also helps connect to the Royal Devon & Exeter Hospital.

The following section of railway round to Plymouth is one of the most famous sections of railway in the world and is very scenic as it follows the legendary Dawlish sea wall section and then at Teignmouth turns inland and over the South Devon banks to Plymouth. The section from Exeter St Davids along the Dawlish sea wall to Newton Abbot and on to Paignton is known as the *Riviera Line* (one of the *Great Scenic Railways of Devon & Cornwall*). Here the River Exe is on our left, but the waterway nearest the railway is the Exeter Canal. This canal runs between the railway and the River Exe for about 5 miles. It was one of the first canals built in England, having been commenced in Queen Elizabeth I's time. Soon to the right the pinnacled tower of Alphington Church is visible. While to the left the ancient seaport of Topsham can be seen across the River Exe.

This is on the Exeter Central to Exmouth railway line. This line can be seen from time to time following the river bank on the other side of the River Exe. On the right is the village of Exminster with a 15th century church containing one of the ornate Devonshire carved screens.

Soon on the right can be seen the village of Powderham with its Church and Belvidere Tower. The Tower is set on a hill with wide views over the estuary of the River Exe. On the left across the River Exe can be seen *Nutwell Court*. The great treasure of this house is a panel from Sir Francis Drake's ship 'The Golden Hind'. Behind can be seen the waterside village of Lympstone.

Next the focus of interest shifts to the right once more as *Powderham Castle*. This is the ancestral home of the Right Hon. The Earl of Devon and is set in its vast deer park. The castle was built about the time of the Norman conquest and has been the home of the Courtenay family since 1377 who have been Earls of Devon since 1533.

Soon the train reaches **Starcross** station and here there is a splendid view across to Exmouth. A notable feature of Starcross is the Italianate pumping engine house which can be seen to the right as we pass Starcross station. It is the best surviving building from Brunel's unsuccessful Atmospheric Railway. This abortive enterprise is commemorated in the "Atmospheric Railway" pub located opposite the railway station. The engine house is now home to the Starcross Sailing & Cruising Club. From Starcross there is a ferry service to Exmouth operated by [Starcross Exmouth Ferry](#) Between here and Exmouth is the vast open stretch of water that is the estuary of the River Exe. Also there is Dawlish Warren a sandbank which thrusts itself out into the Exe like a breakwater at the mouth of the river. At the western end of it is **Dawlish Warren** station, with Langstone Cliff rising up just beyond. Here the railway runs alongside the sea wall and the open sea for the first time. A fine headland that rises on the opposite side of the estuary beyond Exmouth hides from view the seaside town of Budleigh Salterton which lurks just round the corner. Near the station is [Brunel Holiday Park](#) where five railway carriages are camping coaches.

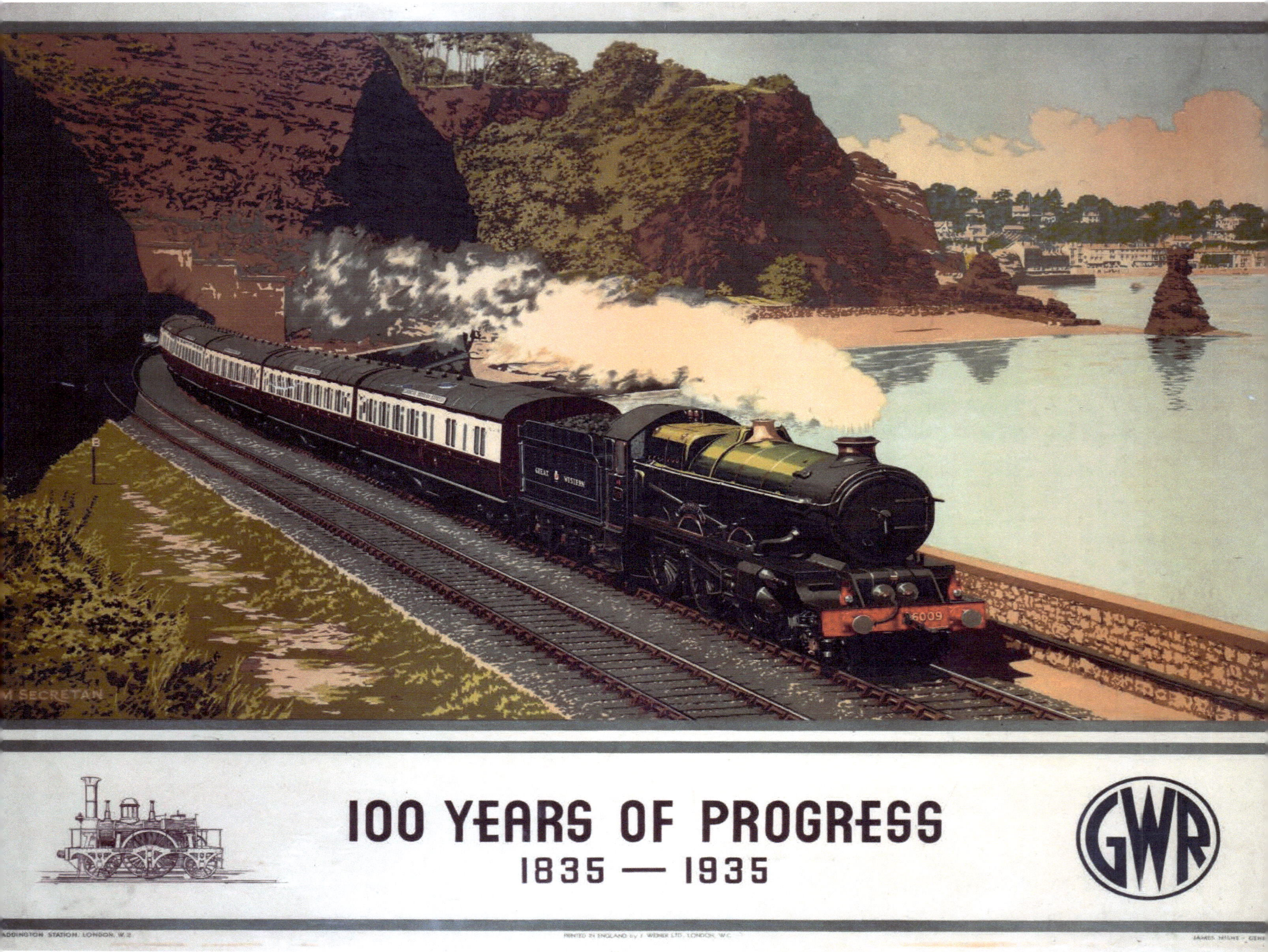

 **100 YEARS OF PROGRESS**

1835 — 1935

Fine red sandstone cliffs rise up on the right as the railway runs alongside the famous Great Western sea wall which continues all the way to Teignmouth. However the next station reached is **Dawlish** and this is the first seaside resort reached on the Cornish Riviera route from London. Dawlish is divided into two distinct parts, the old town on the right with Dawlish Water running through it and the new town. The next section of the line along the famous sea wall is punctuated by the train plunging into tunnels at regular intervals with glimpses of the sea in between. The first tunnel reached is Kennaway Tunnel followed by Phillot Tunnel. Next follows Clerk's Tunnel and then Coryton Tunnel. This is the namesake to Coryton Cove one of the small coves along this stretch of coast. Finally comes Parson's Tunnel the longest and last of the series. On our exit to the left can be seen the Parson & Clerk Rock. If we look back the way we have come at this point we will see the wide expanse of sea to where the Devon coast runs into Dorset in the east and on a fine day you can see all the way to Portland Bill. Today this section of coast is known as the *Jurassic Coast - the Dorset & East Devon Coast World Heritage Site*. Beyond Parson's Tunnel the line reaches the outskirts of Teignmouth a highly picturesque seaside resort and port at the mouth of the River Teign. The Danes raided it hundreds of years ago as did the French in 1690. Here the railway turns inland after a brief glimpse of the seafront and reaches **Teignmouth** station.

After Teignmouth the line follows the River Teign inland and passes the *Port of Teignmouth* before running inland alongside the River Teign. Across the estuary to the left can be seen the village of Shaldon which lies at the waterside in the shadow of Ness Rock. Soon we can see the Teignmouth Bridge which carries the road from Teignmouth to Torquay across the estuary of the River Teign. The village of Bishop's Teignton can be seen on the right had an ancient importance through its close association with the Bishops of Exeter who had a country residence here. The Little Haldon Hills which spread inland from here are the foothills to the vast expanse of Dartmoor. Soon the line passes King's Teignton on the right and across the country to the right can be seen one of the famous Dartmoor tors, Haytor, which is 1,400 ft high and is crowned by a magnificent heap of rocks. Next the railway passes under the A380 main road and *Newton Abbot Racecourse* is passed on the right and a moment later **Newton Abbot** station is reached. Just after the Racecourse is passed the disused former branch line to Heathfield and Moretonhampstead joins the mainline on the right. Near Moretonhampstead was the former Great Western Railway owned hotel *Manor House Hotel (now the Bovey Castle Hotel)*. Newton Abbot is a pleasant town at the head of the Teign estuary and is an important junction for connections to the English Riviera at Torquay and Paignton and it also is a good centre for visiting the *Dartmoor National Park*.

After Newton Abbot station the mainline becomes four tracks as the *Riviera Line* (one of the *Great Scenic Railways of Devon & Cornwall*) to Paignton separates off to the left at Aller Junction. Torquay, Paignton and Brixham centred around Tor Bay are known as the *English Riviera* and the line once continued beyond Paignton to Kingswear (for Dartmouth) however this section of line is now home to the *Dartmouth Steam Railway & Riverboat Company*.

Meanwhile the mainline to Plymouth curves round to the right and starts ascending the steep South Devon banks. On the right can be seen the buildings of the St Augustine's Abbotskerswell Priory, a large modern convent of Canonesses Regular of the Lateran an order with a most interesting history. When the ancient Abbey of Burnham in Buckinghamshire, founded in 1265 was dissolved by King Henry VIII, a nun crossed to Flanders and succeeded in establishing an English convent of the same Order in Louvain in 1609. In 1794 the French Revolution drove the nuns back to England and after living in succession at Hammersmith, Amesbury Abbey in Wiltshire and at Spettisbury in Dorset, the community came to Newton Abbot in 1861 and the Priory ceased in 1983. It has now been converted into flats as the *Priory* retirement village. The convent which has a magnificent church, thus forms an interesting link to pre-Reformation England. The village seen beyond the Priory is Abbots Kerswell in the name of which there is an obvious harking back to ancient monastic associations. The name distinguishes it from Kingkerswell which is a village on the left and which has a station on the Torbay line.

The line then climbs steeply up Dainton bank between the rugged cliffs and quarry workings in the red and pink stone of Dainton Hill until Dainton Tunnel is reached at the summit. Then the view opens out again. Looking up the valley to the right, a long succession of views of Dartmoor can be seen, with distant tors showing their rocky crests in silhouette on the skyline. On the right also appears the village of Littlehempston identified by the lofty tower of its ancient church. The former Ashburton branch line then can be seen joining the mainline on the right. This branch is now home to the *South Devon Railway* and their station at Totnes Riverside can be seen on the right on the approach to **Totnes** station. From Totnes Rail Station and *Totnes Royal Seven Stars Hotel* there are bus links to Dartmouth, Kingsbridge and Salcombe. *Totnes Rare Breeds Farm* is located near Totnes Riverside. On the left you can get a glimpse of the town of Totnes and *Totnes Castle* perched up high above the town. This occupies the highest point in Totnes and dominates the town. The building of it is attributed to a Norman baron named Judhael who came to England with the Norman conquest, but probably additions to it were made at later periods. *Dartmouth Steam Railway & Riverboats Company* also operates a regular *Totnes to Dartmouth River Cruise* and the multimodal *Round Robin Tour*. Totnes is a picturesque old town and another excellent centre for exploring the *Dartmoor National Park* and the River Dart. In 2006 Totnes become the first *transition town* of the transition initiative. In March 2007 Totnes was the first town in Britain to introduce its own local alternative currency, the Totnes Pound, to support the local economy of the town. Due to increasing contactless payments the Totnes Pound was discontinued in 2019.

> **SOUTH DEVON RAILWAY:**
>
> The South Devon Railway is a heritage steam railway that offers 7 miles of heritage railway along the stunning valley of the River Dart between Buckfastleigh and Totnes Riverside. Totnes Riverside station is a short walk from the Totnes mainline rail station.
>
> The line was originally the Ashburton branch but sadly in 1971, the line from Buckfastleigh to Ashburton was lost to the widening of the A38. Today it is one of the best recreations of a classic GWR rural branch line. It has a fine collection of GWR steam locomotives and carriages. The museum at Buckfastleigh is home to an original broad gauge steam locomotive "No 151 Tiny" which was built in 1868 for the original South Devon Railway.
>
> Website: https://www.southdevonrailway.co.uk/

A little further on again on the left hand side can be seen Follaton House (now offices of South Hams District Council). After Totnes the line continues winding through the landscape with hills rising steeply on either side, the country on the right being part of the vast expanse of Dartmoor. Soon the village of Tigley can be seen on the right with its church as the train ascends the steep Rattery bank. A little further inland on the right can be seen the village of Rattery marked by its church steeple. The church here is one of those that have helped make Devon famous for its carved oak screens. On the left the Harbourne River follows the railway. After crossing this river the railway plunges into Marley Tunnel and after emerging there is a good view of Brent Hill to the right. Soon we pass the village of South Brent, to the south of which the main A38 road can be seen wending its way westwards. Beyond South Brent some of the prominent heights of the southern fringe of Dartmoor can be seen ahead. Amongst these is Ugborough Beacon seen first from the left hand side of the train at South Brent and then on the right as the railway curves round to the south. At the crossing of the little Glaze Brook there is a brief glimpse up the valley to the long ridge of Ugborough Moor. On the right the village of Wrangaton can be seen while to the left is the A38 main road. This is the location of the steep Wrangaton bank for trains going eastbound. On the right is the village of Bittaford. Soon the sight of Western Beacon greets us on the right hand side as the train reaches **Ivybridge** station. We cross the wooded valley of the River Erme and the village of Ivybridge can be seen on the left. A fine expanse of landscape opens out to the left as we leave the Erme Valley at Ivybridge and travel towards the Yealm Valley which runs parallel with it a few miles further west. On the right, Henlake Down and Hangar Down rise close together.

The railway now crosses the River Yealm and comes down through Cornwood and splendid views open up to the right looking north to Penn Moor and Lee Moor. Penn Beacon rises up above. On the right soon after crossing Piall River is Beechwood Park, and a little further on again on the right is *Hemerdon House*. Just behind it is Hemerdon Ball a hill where a big camp was established in the Napoleonic wars. This is the location of the steep Hemerdon bank for trains going eastbound. The village to the left of the railway is Ridgeway. Now we cross Tory Brook which comes down from Penn Moor and pass through Plympton, an ancient town now subsumed into the suburbs of Plymouth. Plympton's claim to fame is that Sir Joshua Reynolds was born here in 1723.

The railway then passes under the A38 main road and begins the approach to Plymouth. The River Plym is soon seen on the left and we pass the train depot at Laira and the triangle of lines where the line to Plymouth Friary branches off to the left. Plymouth Friary was once the terminus of Southern Railway trains from London Waterloo which had arrived in Plymouth from Exeter via Okehampton and Tavistock before passing eastwards through Plymouth North Road station and arriving at Plymouth Friary. Finally we pass through Mutley Tunnel and enter **Plymouth North Road** station. At Plymouth there is the *Dartmoor Explorer* bus service to Exeter via Yelverton, Princetown and Moretonhampstead across Dartmoor.

[Plymouth is Britain's Ocean City](#) and has the history of England and the British Empire written all over it. Here Sir Francis Drake played bowls on Plymouth Hoe while waiting for the Spanish Armada. In 1620, the Pilgrim Fathers departed Plymouth for the New World on board the Mayflower and established Plymouth Colony, the second English settlement in what is now the United States of America. This story is now celebrated in the [Mayflower Museum](#). Plymouth is also home to the great [HM Naval Base Devonport](#) which is the largest operational naval base in Western Europe. In 1919 Nancy Astor was elected the first-ever female member of parliament to take office in the British Houses of Parliament for the constituency of Plymouth Sutton. Sadly Plymouth got very heavily bombed during the Second World War and underwent extensive reconstruction in the postwar years. Today only in the area around the Barbican can you see any of the medieval architecture that once dominated this fine city. The sweeping boulevard that is the Armada Way takes you down from the station in a straight line to the Hoe and a spectacular view of the famous Plymouth Sound. Plymouth is also home to the world renowned [Plymouth Marine Laboratory](#), [Smart Sound Plymouth](#) and the [National Marine Aquarium](#). The [Plymouth Gin Distillery](#) has been producing Plymouth Gin since 1793, which was exported around the world by the Royal Navy. [The Box Plymouth](#) is the city's major new museum and art gallery and opened in 2020. Plymouth is also the departure point for the [Brittany Ferries](#) services to Roscoff in France and Santander in Spain. These ferry sailings depart from the [ABP Plymouth](#)'s Continental Ferry Terminal in [Millbay Docks](#). Plymouth is also home to the [Plymouth and South Devon Freeport](#). The prestigious [Duke of Cornwall Hotel](#) is located near Millbay Docks and was built to serve ocean liners.

The city overlooks the natural sheltered harbour and anchorages of [Plymouth Sound National Marine Park](#), protected by the [Royal Citadel](#) built by King Charles II. Standing on the Hoe is the iconic [Smeaton's Tower](#) lighthouse. Gaze down at the shoreline and you'll see the glorious [Tinside Lido](#), open to the public for bathing during the summer months. The scenic Hoe Promenade is where Sir Francis Drake played his famous game of bowls before commanding the English fleet against the Spanish Armada. The Elizabethan [Barbican Waterfront](#), [Cattewater Harbour](#) and [Sutton Harbour](#), where many buildings remain little changed since they were constructed in the 16th Century, is home to the Mayflower Steps, from where the Pilgrim Fathers embarked for their departure to the New World in 1620. The area remains home to Plymouth's fishing fleet and combines the charm of Elizabethan England with modern visitor facilities, including art galleries, shops, restaurants, cafes and waterside pubs. [Millbay Docks](#) and [Royal William Yard](#) are other waterfront quarters of Plymouth. [Plymouth Boat Trips](#) operate a variety of ferries and cruises around Plymouth Sound, River Lynher, River Yealm and River Tamar. The location is ideally suited for exploring the beautiful coves and inlets of Devon and Cornwall, as well as the rugged beauty of [Dartmoor National Park](#). You can explore the [Drakes Trail](#) walking & cycling route that links Plymouth with Tavistock. Notable hotels in Plymouth include the [Duke of Cornwall Hotel](#), [New Continental Hotel](#) and the [Crowne Plaza Plymouth](#).

Plymouth also marks the end of an important stage of the journey on the Cornish Riviera Express route from London to Penzance as after Plymouth the train leaves Devon and crosses the River Tamar to enter Cornwall on its last leg to Penzance.

FUN FACT: DID YOU KNOW THAT…..

In 1919 Nancy Astor became the first woman Member of Parliament, representing the constituency of Sutton in Plymouth.

FUN FACT: DID YOU KNOW THAT……

The original Eddystone Lighthouse (1698 - 1703) was the first offshore lighthouse in the world and constructed of wood. The third Eddystone Lighthouse was re-erected on Plymouth Hoe in 1882 and is a now popular tourist attraction. The fourth Eddystone Lighthouse is still in use.

FUN FACT: DID YOU KNOW THAT…..

Sir Francis Chichester left Plymouth on 27 August 1966 in his ketch Gipsy Moth IV and circumnavigated the world singlehanded, arriving back in Plymouth on 28 May 1967 after 266 days.

FUN FACT: DID YOU KNOW THAT……

The oldest commercial bakery IN THE ENTIRE WORLD can be found in Plymouth! You'll find it on the Barbican, Jackas Bakery is thought to be the oldest bakery in the world that is still in operation and dates back to 1600! It is thought that the biscuits that were taken on the Mayflower in 1620 were made there!

FUN FACT: DID YOU KNOW THAT…..

Plymouth also boasts England's oldest working distillery, Plymouth Gin, where you can still buy Plymouth Original Strength Gin! The distillery is located in the Barbican and their gins have been in production, made to the original recipe since the 1700s!

Website: https://www.plymouthgin.com/

FUN FACT: DID YOU KNOW THAT……

Plymouth Tea, a local tea merchant based in Plymouth, has Devon's first tea plantation, growing on the banks of the River Tavy. This is only the second tea plantation in England after the one at Tregothan in Cornwall.

Website: https://www.plymouthtea.co.uk/

FUN FACT: DID YOU KNOW THAT……

Plympton-born 18th century portrait artist Sir Joshua Reynolds (1723-1792) was the founding President of the Royal Academy, Painter to the King, a published author, art collector and Knight of the Realm.

FUN FACT: DID YOU KNOW THAT……

Sir Francis Drake circumnavigated the world in 1577 starting out from Plymouth. It took him 3 years to complete sailing against the winds and the tides. A statue commemorating this famous voyage now stands on Plymouth Hoe.

FUN FACT: DID YOU KNOW THAT……

The Pilgrim Fathers famously departed from Plymouth on board the Mayflower in 1620 bound for the New World. The men and women on board braved the hardships of life at sea to set up the second English colony in North America in Plymouth (Massachussetts). This colony helped to establish trade and gave England a presence in the Americas. Today it is known as the United States of America and the Mayflower continues to be celebrated as part of its founding story.

FUN FACT: DID YOU KNOW THAT……

Charles Darwin's voyage on the HMS Beagle which helped him confirm his theory of evolution set sail from Plymouth in Dec 1831.

FUN FACT: DID YOU KNOW THAT……

Plymouth has the oldest Ashkenazi Synagogue in continuous use in the English speaking world which dates from 1762.

FUN FACT: DID YOU KNOW THAT……

Dame Agnes Weston (1840-1918) was famed for championing sailor welfare and she set up the first Royal Sailor's Rest in Plymouth as a club for RN sailors. Aggie's faith and dedication led to the Sailor's Rests becoming a phenomenon, with presence in all the main naval bases, including several abroad. She was known to all sailors as The Sailor's Friend or more commonly and affectionately as Aggie. She was the first woman to be given a full ceremonial Royal Navy funeral. A blue plaque was unveiled in her honour in 2021. Her legacy continues with the "Aggies" charity which she founded in 1876.

https://www.aggies.org.uk

FUN FACT: DID YOU KNOW THAT……

Plymouth Marine Laboratory maintains the Western Channel Observatory which is globally renowned for being one of the most comprehensive and longest established sea shelf observatories in the world.

FUN FACT: DID YOU KNOW THAT……

Plymouth has a strong sailing and yachting heritage. It has been the finishing point for the famed Fastnet yachting race since it started in 1925. Also the renowned Port of Plymouth Sailing Regatta is one of the oldest sailing regattas in the world having started in 1823.

FUN FACT: DID YOU KNOW THAT……

In 1768, 1772 and 1776 Captain James Cook set sail from Plymouth on his three famous voyages of discovery that mapped and explored the Pacific Ocean and discovered Tasmania, Hawaii and New Zealand for the first time for European people. Indigenous people from the Pacific and Polynesia, of course, had been living there for centuries so already knew about these places!

FUN FACT: DID YOU KNOW THAT……

Legend has it that Sir Francis Drake was told of the first sighting of the Spanish Armada off the English Coast while playing a game of bowls on Plymouth Hoe. He finished the game and went on to resoundingly defeat the Spanish with the English Navy. The Spanish Armada set sail from Spain in July 1588, with the mission of overthrowing England's Queen Elizabeth I who was a Protestant and restoring Catholic rule over England. The Spanish Armada was the defining moment of Queen Elizabeth I's reign and was commemorated in the famed Armada Portrait which is now permanently displayed at the Queen's House in Greenwich - the birthplace of Queen Elizabeth I. Spain's defeat secured Protestant rule in England and launched Queen Elizabeth I onto the global stage marking the start of England's rise to global prominence. It remains one of the most legendary and iconic moments of British history.

Plymouth to Penzance:

On leaving Plymouth North Road station the line bends round to the right and soon the train reaches **Devonport** station. The great naval base of Devonport joins Plymouth to the west and the famous dockyards of the Royal Navy stretch for a couple of miles along the Hamoaze, which is the broad estuary through which the Rivers Tamar, Tavy and Lynher find their way into Plymouth Sound.

Devonport has long been a major base for the Royal Navy and has been a naval base for centuries. [Devonport Naval Base](#) is the largest naval base in Western Europe and covers over 650 acres and has 15 dry docks, four miles of waterfront, 25 tidal basins and 5 basins. For many years each of the Royal Navy's naval bases hosted "Navy Days", this tradition was continued by the biennial Plymouth Navy Days held at Devonport. Navy Days were restyled as the "Meet Your Navy" event in 2008 and Devonport Naval Base regularly hosted the biennial celebrations in alternation with Portsmouth Naval Base. Today part of Devonport South Yard is now regenerated as [Oceansgate Plymouth](#) and home to [Princess Yachts](#) superyacht manufacturer as well as the preserved [HMS Courageous nuclear submarine and the Devonport Naval Heritage Centre](#).

Soon after **Devonport Dockyard** station the line leaps high above Devonport on a great viaduct to the left there are fine views of the Naval Base, there are further great views to the left as the train reaches **Keyham** station. Across the Hamoaze can be seen the village of Torpoint in Cornwall which is connected to Devonport with the [Torpoint Ferry](#). This is our first sight of Cornwall. Torpoint forms a peninsular between the Lynher or St German's River and the sea. Next the [Tamar Valley Line](#) to Bere Alston and Gunnislake (one of the [Great Scenic Railways of Devon & Cornwall](#)) can be seen diverging from the mainline to the right. This is also the remains of the former Southern Railway mainline via Bere Alston, Tavistock and Okehampton to Exeter. Sadly only the section from Plymouth to Bere Alston and Gunnislake remains. From Bere Alston and Calstock you can link with the [Tamara Coast to Coast Way](#) walking trail which takes you to Bude on the North Coast of Cornwall. On the left can be seen views of the approach to the Royal Albert Bridge. Then we pass through **St Budeaux Ferry Road** station and then pass over the Gunnislake branch and leap on to the famous Royal Albert Bridge to cross the River Tamar just before it joins the St German's River to form the Hamoaze.

The [Royal Albert Bridge](#) at Saltash, was built for the sole purpose of carrying the Great Western Railway across the River Tamar at the expanse of water known as the Hamoaze which forms the narrowest point. It was named in honour of Queen Victoria's husband, Prince Albert, the Prince Consort. It is one of the great engineering masterpieces of Isambard Kingdom Brunel, who constructed the Great Western Railway, and ranks alongside the Forth Bridge and Tay Bridge as one of the most daring and spectacular pieces of engineering in the world. It was first opened in 1859 and the two main spans are each of 445 feet and there are 17 smaller spans of about 69 ft each. The total length of the bridge is 2,240 ft and the bridge is 100ft above the waters of the River Tamar. Above the entrance arches as the train moves onto the bridge can be read the words:

I.K. Brunel

Engineer

1859

As the train crosses the Hamoaze at the height of 100ft above high water level, you gain magnificent views of the estuary to the left and the [Tamar Road Bridge](#) to the right and the Tamar Valley beyond.

The Tamar Road Bridge is in public ownership, being owned and operated jointly by Cornwall Council and Plymouth City Council. It is notable as the first significant post-war suspension bridge, and the longest ever in the UK. The Tamar Road Bridge was opened to the public on 24th October 1961, and was formally opened by the Queen Elizabeth the Queen Mother on 26th April 1962 in a grand ceremony involving a fly-past and two naval frigates. Established to celebrate the engineering legacy of the Tamar Estuary's historic bridges, the [Bridging the Tamar Visitor and Learning Centre](#) opened in Spring 2019. The Visitor and Learning Centre interprets the heritage of both the 20th century Tamar Road Bridge and Brunel's iconic 19th century Royal Albert Bridge.

Below there is also the [Torpoint Ferries](#) which are a chain ferry between Devonport and Torpoint across the Hamoaze. The Torpoint Ferry crossing is the busiest estuarial vehicular ferry crossing in the United Kingdom, and the three vessels together carry nearly two million vehicles per annum. It is owned and operated jointly by Cornwall Council and Plymouth City Council.

Centenary
1859 — 1959
ROYAL ALBERT BRIDGE, SALTASH
WESTERN REGION — DESIGNED AND BUILT BY ISAMBARD KINGDOM BRUNEL — **WESTERN REGION**

At the far end of the Royal Albert Bridge is **Saltash** and we have now arrived in Cornwall. On the right can be seen the tower of Trematon Castle which dates in part from the 13th century. The most interesting thing about it is that Sir Richard Grenville was once its governor. To the left across the broad estuary of the St German's River or the Lynher River, which flows into the Hamoaze just below Saltash, can be seen Antony House in its parkland. This is the ancient seat of the Carews and Richard Carew who wrote a "Survey of Cornwall" in Elizabethan times is buried in the Anthony Church, a 15th century building, the embattled tower of which can be seen rising from the village which lies to the west of the park. Anchored in the Lynher River can also be seen the former HMS Brecon which since 2008 is now a training ship for HMS Raleigh shore establishment for the Royal Navy.

FUN FACT: DID YOU KNOW THAT……

HMS Brecon (M29) was built in 1978 by Vosper Thornycroft shipyard at Woolston in Southampton for the Royal Navy as a Hunt class mine counter-measures ship (MCMV). She was launched by the Duchess of Kent in June 1978. She was commissioned into service by the Duchess of Kent on 21 March 1980 at Portsmouth. She was the largest ship in the world built of glass reinforced plastic and was the first of the new Hunt class MCMV ships.

She served in the First MCM Squadron from 1980 based out of HM Naval Base Clyde at Faslane and toured around the world on various deployments. She served in the aftermath of the Falklands War (1982) and in the Gulf War (1991). In 1998 she served in the Northern Ireland Squadron as a patrol ship. In 1999 she acted as ceremonial guardship for the Tall Ships Race when it visited Greenock.

Notably, HMS Brecon was the first Royal Navy ship ever to be commanded by a woman. Lieutenant Charlotte "Charlie" Atkinson became her last commanding officer in January 2004. She was finally retired and decommissioned from Royal Navy service on 19 July 2005. In her operational career she had steamed 339,244 nautical miles and visited 105 ports and 28 countries around the world. She was released from duty on 30 Sep 2005.

Since February 2008 she has become a static training ship for HMS Raleigh shore establishment of the Royal Navy at Devonport in Plymouth and is moored in the River Lynher near Saltash in Cornwall as a seamanship classroom to give new recruits their first experiences and taste of life on board a Royal Navy warship.

The train now dives into Shillingham Tunnel and on emerging to the right if you look across the country you can see the rounded summit of Kit Hill. At a point due south of Kit Hill, the railway crosses the River Lynher and then the River Tiddy then the line enters **St German's** station. Adjacent to the rail station are some old railway carriages now converted into holiday accommodation by [Rail Holidays](). The town of St German's is a small town which was an ancient borough until the time of the Reform Act. Its fine Norman Church is not visible from the railway but the tower of St Erny Church can be seen across country to the right.

In passing through St German's the trees of [Port Eliot Park](), the ancestral home of the Right Hon. The Earl of St German's, can be seen on the right. When the train is clear of the town, Kit Hill shows up again. A little beyond and to the west of it is seen the tower of Landrake Church, while in the far distance looking right across the Devonshire border to the north is a fine view of Dartmoor. Now looking to the right again ahead there is the steeple of Menheniot Church, where the famous William of Wykeham was once the Rector. While the high country seen to the right forms the outskirts of Bodmin Moor.

We are now in a land of hills separated by winding, zigzagging valleys which the train crosses in quick succession by frequent viaducts. We are now passing the fringe of the vast expanse of Bodmin Moor. The train then crosses the River Seaton, which comes down from the moorland country to the north and flows here between well wooded banks, just before we pass **Menheniot** station.

Clicker Tor is a small hill to the left with a fine silhouette of jagged rocks on its crest. The Tor rises close beside the railway and as the line curves round we see it from different angles. A while after Menheniot station the line passes under the A38 main road. Soon we reach **Liskeard** station. Liskeard church can be seen to the right as we approach the town. The church is the second largest in Cornwall.

Liskeard is a typical Cornish town set at the edge of the vast uplands of Bodmin Moor. The Cheesewring is a weird pile of rocks no less mysterious than Stonehenge. In this same area are the mysterious Dogmare Poole set at the highest point of the moors; the Trevethy Stone; the Hurlers, which are relics of ancient stone circles.

At right angles to Liskeard station is the station for the [Looe Valley Line]() (one of the [Great Scenic Railways of Devon & Cornwall]()) which then climbs down underneath the mainline before it can be seen to the left of the mainline reversing at Coombe and then continuing its sinuous way down to the coast at Looe. Soon after Liskeard station the mainline crosses the River Looe just above the village of Lamellion.

For the next few miles the right hand side of the line offers the most interesting country, with fine views of Bodmin Moor opening up at intervals as the train crosses the valleys. The tower of St Cleer Church rising out of the landscape to the north, makes a landmark to the right as we leave Liskeard. Both the railway and the A38 main road then enter the valley of the River Fowey and the three run close together for the next couple of miles.

The charming river flowing between wooded banks, joins the line close to Doublebois. At this point the river is joined by a tributary that comes down from the north through another wooded vale and flows close to Treverbyn Vean seen on the right of the railway just beyond the meeting of the two streams at a point called Two Waters Foot.

A couple of miles across country to the left, beyond the lovely Larynn Woods, which clothe the Fowey Valley on this side, is Braddock Down, the scene of a battle fought on the 19th January 1643 between a Royalist force led by Sir Ralph Hopton and Sir Bevil Grenville and a portion of the Roundhead garrison of Plymouth, which had marched out here under Ruthven, the governor of the port for the Parliament. In this engagement the Royalists won a decisive victory.

On each side of the railway are ancient barrows, entrenchments and earthworks. The River Fowey which the railway follows closely here is one of the most delightful of Cornish streams, coming down from the high lands of *Bodmin Moor* and giving itself to the sea at the attractive little coastal resort of Fowey. Beyond Lewarne on the right a little stream finds its way through Well Wood and enters the River Fowey. Here the railway curves through the wooded valley and the A38 main road heads off on its way to the right towards Bodmin. Soon the railway reaches **Bodmin Parkway** station. Here there are bus links to Bodmin, Wadebridge and Padstow (see *Transport for Cornwall* for more information). Padstow is centred on the beautiful *Camel Estuary* and *Trevose Head*. It is famous food destination with its *Rick Stein* restaurants, cookery school and shops. Near the station is *Lanhydrock House*. Just after the station the branch line to Bodmin General curves off to the right and is now home to the *Bodmin & Wenford Railway*.

BODMIN RAILWAY:

The Bodmin Railway is Cornwall's only heritage steam railway. Relax in style and enjoy a leisurely 13-mile round trip through beautiful Cornish countryside, taking in the sights, sounds and smells of a bygone age, as the era of a Cornish branch line in the 1950s reveals itself during the course of your journey.

Trains operate from Bodmin General, the principal station where free coach and car parking is available, to both Bodmin Parkway station – where connections can be made directly with main line railway services – and Boscarne Junction, which is situated directly adjacent to the Camel Trail recreational footpath and cycle way.

Website: https://bodminrailway.co.uk/

LANHYDROCK HOUSE:

This magnificent late Victorian country house stands in extensive grounds above the River Fowey. When visiting the house you can discover the two sides of a country house including the "upstairs living" of the luxurious family areas and bedrooms to the "below stairs living" of the servants areas and the kitchen. There are also beautiful gardens to explore. It has been owned and managed by the National Trust since 1953.

Website: https://www.nationaltrust.org.uk/visit/cornwall/lanhydrock

The town of Bodmin lies to the north west of Bodmin Parkway station. After leaving Bodmin Parkway the railway passes through the short Brown Queen Tunnel and curves round through the wooded valley, still keeping close to the river, before we pass the magnificent ruins of [Restormel Castle](#) to the right. The castle which has been in ruins for many centuries now is believed to have been built by the Cardenham family at the time of King Edward I. It was at one time the residence of the Earls of Cornwall and now forms part of the [Duchy of Cornwall](#)'s property. The Duke of Cornwall, Duke of Rothesay and Earl of Chester are some of the titles held automatically by the Prince of Wales as heir to the British throne. Opposite Restormel is Druid's Hill visible on the left with a cross on its summit.

Beyond Restormel the line reaches the ancient town of Lostwithiel lying in the valley of the Fowey. **Lostwithiel** station was the junction for the Fowey branch, now a freight only line, which bears off to the left after the station and follows the river down to its estuary at Fowey. [Fowey Harbour](#) is an important port for the export of china clay around the world from Cornwall's china clay mines. These china clay mines are now operated by [Imerys](#). The mainline crosses the river and then bids farewell to the Fowey Valley before striking across the moors on a short cut to the coast. Beyond Treverran Tunnel the tower of Tywardreath Church appears on the left and beyond the village is [Trenython House](#) set high up amid the woodlands. On the other side of the line to the right is the china clay mining town of St Blazey. At **Par** station the [Atlantic Coast Line](#) (one of the [Great Scenic Railways of Devon & Cornwall](#)) which goes to St Blazey and then across Cornwall to the seaside and surfing resort of Newquay can be see diverging from the mainline to the right just after the station.

Just beyond Par station the railway skirts the edge of Par Sands and the [Imery's owned Par Harbour](#) which is busy with the export of china clay around the world from Cornwall's china clay mines. These china clay mines are now operated by [Imerys](#). Beyond it we have a view of the sea at [St Austell Bay](#). Now the railway hugs the coastline and looking across the bay to the left near Par Harbour we gain a good view of Gribbin Head, which juts out into the Channel between the mouth of the Fowey and St Austell Bay. Fowey is out of sight just round the corner to the east. The corresponding headland at the western end of the bay is Black Head.

Looking inland to the right can be seen the village of St Blazey Gate. After passing St Blazey Gate the railway gradually draws away from the sea as it approaches St Austell still the chief centre of the china clay industry in Cornwall. Its great granite church on the left is one of the most ornate in Cornwall. Soon **St Austell** station is reached. Here there are bus links to the world famous [Eden Project](#) and its huge tropical biomes housed in a former china clay pit. There are also bus links to the [Lost Gardens of Heligan](#) and Mevagissey. There are also bus links to Charlestown (for [Charlestown Harbour](#) and the [Shipwreck Treasure Museum](#)) and Fowey. See [Transport for Cornwall](#) for more information on bus connections. Between Fowey and Mevagissey there is a passenger ferry [Mevagissey Ferries](#).

THE EDEN PROJECT:

Dubbed the Eighth Wonder of the World by some, Eden Project is a dramatic global garden housed in tropical biomes that nestle in a former china clay pit near St Austell. It was founded by Sir Tim Smit KBE and Jonathan Ball and opened in 2001.

"*Eden Project put simply is an attitude. It is that if good people come together at one point you can take something that is apparently hopeless and transform it into something that is full of hope. And in so doing you excite people all over the place to go and do their own version of things that are hopeful. So, I guess that we are a catalyst. I really believe in people. You scratch the surface and underneath this I reckon that 99% of the whole population of this wonderful planet of ours is good. I don't think we have scratched the surface of what we are capable of. I think we are just on the start of a journey*." Sir Tim Smit KBE (Co-Founder of the Eden Project)

Eden is a feast for the senses and can be experienced in so many different ways, whether you're looking for calming immersion in nature or a fun-packed day of adventure. Begin your journey in the Outdoor Gardens, where wild landscapes are juxtaposed with Europe's largest collection of useful plants – from food crops to medicines – alongside striking colour-themed borders. Experience the sights and scents of the Mediterranean Biome, where you'll find beautiful flower displays and ripening seasonal crops. Then immerse yourself in the steamy heat of the Rainforest Biome, the gleaming green jewel in Eden's crown. Here you can marvel at the breathtaking view of the treetops from the Canopy Walkway.

Website: https://www.edenproject.com/

Beyond St Austell the line skirts the edge of Sparnon Moor which banks up on the right. Beyond is Burngullow Common now filled with dumps of china clay. To the right can be seen some extensive china clay workings and a freight line can be seen diverging from the mainline to the right serving these china clay areas.

Now we cross the River Fal and on the right is Trenowth Wood. A lot of places in Cornwall begin with 'Tre'. No less than 224 towns, villages and hamlets in the county start their names in this fashion. The reason for this is that in the ancient Cornish language 'tre' means homestead or town-place.

The contours of an ancient camp can be seen on a hill to the right before passing through the village of Grampound Road. Soon on the left we pass the village of Probus and its church. Its tower is said to be the tallest and most beautiful in Cornwall. Soon the train speeds through Polperro Tunnel and Buckshead Tunnel. Soon views of the city of Truro are seen to the left as the railway enters the city high on a viaduct and the three lofty towers of *Truro Cathedral* can be seen dominating the city. This was the first Gothic cathedral completed in England since the Reformation and was begun in 1880 and the exterior was completed in 1912. **Truro** station is the junction for the *Maritime Line* to Falmouth (one of the *Great Scenic Railways of Devon & Cornwall*) which can be seen branching off to the left soon after leaving Truro and it crosses Penwithers Viaduct. At the heart of Truro is *Lemon Quay Market* and the Bus Station. See *Transport for Cornwall* for more information on bus connections.

On leaving Truro the train enters the chief mining district of Cornwall with disused mine chimneys and engine houses dotting the landscape. Soon the village of Chacewater is passed. Chacewater has its place in engineering history, for it was in a mine here that Watt's first pumping engine was erected. The A30 main road then rejoins the railway and runs alongside it to the right. At Scorrier to the south lies the mansion *Scorrier House* hidden in woodland. Meanwhile St Agnes Beacon can be seen rising to the right and then there is a glimpse of Portreath and the North Cornish coast. In the middle distance is the mining village of Illogan whose church tower set on a hill serves as a useful landmark for mariners.

Soon we reach **Redruth** station. Here there are bus links to Helston and the Lizard. At the Lizard you can visit *Lizard Point* and the famous *Lizard Lighthouse* which marks the most southerly location in mainland Britain. There is also *Godolphin House* near Helston which is managed by the National Trust. See *Transport for Cornwall* for more information on bus connections from Redruth.

Redruth presents us with the legacy of the industrial aspect of Cornish life with its iron foundries and tin smelting works. While the surrounding countryside is also heavily scored with the legacy of tin and copper mining. Many of the historic remnants of the Cornish Mining industry are now part of the *Cornwall & West Devon Mining World Heritage Site*. In the town is the house in which gas was used for lighting for the first time in England as the invention of William Murdock. That was in 1792 and an inscription on the house, which was Murdock's home, credits him with having made and tested the first steam locomotive here in 1784.

Soon we pass the rocky foot of Carn Brea hill on the left. Many ancient relics have been found here as it was one of the great fortified places in Cornwall in pre-Roman times. The Monument is the form of a Celtic cross commemorates Lord de Dunstanville. Close to the railway on the right soon after Carn Brea are the disused mine workings of the famous Dolcoath Mine, once one of the richest of the Cornish tin and copper mines before the decline of the industry. It is nearly 3000 ft deep.

Camborne is the next station reached and the town is a mining town of similar character to Redruth. To the left rise the peaks of Godolphin Hill and Treginning Hill. Both hills are littered with relics of the tin and copper mines that once dominated this area.

Soon the port of Hayle is reached and **Hayle** station. Adjacent to the rail station are some old railway carriages now converted into holiday accommodation by *Rail Holidays*. From the broad estuary of the Hayle River rise two loft towers of steel girder work carrying electric mains across the river. Here we have a good view into St Ives Bay and a passing glimpse of St Ives. On the western bank of the Hayle estuary can be seen the fine tower of Lelant Church. The famous *West Cornwall Golf Course* can be seen on the far side of the estuary just above the village of Lelant. Carnsew Reservoir is part of *Hayle Harbour*. Water is stored here at high tide and frequently allowed to escape with a rush to scour the harbour channel.

At **St Erth** station the *St Ives Bay Line* (one of the *Great Scenic Railways of Devon & Cornwall*) can be seen heading off to the coast via Lelant to the left just before entering the station. St Erth Village lies just a short distance from the railway to the left. Across the country to the right is Trencrom Hill rumoured in Cornish legend to be the home of giants. Ludgvan Village, with a 14th century church tower, soon appears on the right. Apparently the last native wolf in England was killed here. Soon the railway meets the coast at Marazion. While approaching Marazion you catch a first glimpse of the amazing sight of *St Michael's Mount* rising up out of Mount's Bay. On the pinnacle of rock a monastery was established before the Norman Conquest. Now the castle that crowns this rocky outcrop is the ancestral home of Lord St Levan. For most of the day and night the sea divides the Mount from Marazion but at each tide it is possible to walk across via the causeway during a period of about 4 hours. When the tide is in then ferry services are available from Marazion in summer only.

With the amazing sight of St Michael's Mount in view that means that we are now only a few miles from journeys end. Already Penzance can be seen straight ahead, while a little to the left can be seen Newlyn, a charming little resort on Gwavas Lake which is a tiny bay. Behind it and to the left rise the hills stretching round westwards to Land's End. To the right the A394 main road accompanies the railway into Penzance and Long Rock train depot is passed on the right.

To the south of Newlyn, the small St Clement's Isle stands a little way out to sea in front of Mousehole and the church of Paul is seen on the skyline. Drawing nearer to Penzance we may look out back across the broad sweep of Mount's Bay towards the Lizard Peninsular and Poldhu. The historic and pioneering site of Poldhu Point became the site of one of the main technological advances of the early twentieth century when, on 12 December 1901, a wireless signal was sent by Thomas Barron in Poldhu to St John's, Newfoundland, and received by Marconi. The site is famous as the location of Marconi Centre Poldhu and Marconi on the Lizard. Guglielmo Marconi's transmitter for the first transatlantic radio message on 12 December 1901. Marconi received the transmission on Signal Hill, St. John's, Newfoundland. The technology was a precursor to radio, television, satellites and the internet, with the Goonhilly Earth Station at Goonhilly Downs a nearby example. PK Porthcurno – Museum of Global Communications celebrates Cornwall's pioneering role in this technology and the telecommunications revolution.

But now the train draws into **Penzance** station at the end of its long journey from London and comes to a rest at the long platforms of Penzance station with the front of the train nosing under the arched roof over the buffer stops. The Cornish Riviera route from London to Penzance is complete and you have reached Cornwall and the Cornish Riviera. This route from London Paddington to Penzance is also served by the famed Night Riviera Sleeper.

Penzance groups itself finely above the sea. On leaving the station Penzance Harbour greets us outside the station and from there you can board the Isles of Scilly Steamship Company ferry service to the Isles of Scilly on board RMV Scillonian III. Although the RMV Scillonian III will be retired from service after the 2026 operating season and from 2027 will be replaced by the new RMV Scillonian IV. The Penzance Dry Dock is also an important shipyard. Penzance Helicopters also offer services to the Isles of Scilly from their heliport in Penzance. The Isles of Scilly Steamship Company also operate Skybus flights to the Isles of Scilly from their Land's End Airport as well as from Cornwall Newquay Airport and Exeter Airport.

There are also bus links from the adjacent bus station, including Transport for Cornwall open top services to Land's End, operating clockwise via Newlyn and Porthcurno, where the Minack Theatre and PK Porthcurno – Museum of Global Communications are located, or anti clockwise via Marazion and St Ives.). Transport for Cornwall also operates open top services to St Just and Pendeen, where the Geevor Tin Mine Museum is located, which is part of the Cornish Mining World Heritage Site.

[Newlyn Harbour](#) is one of the major fishing ports in the South West. Penzance is home to the new [Newlyn Art Gallery](#) establishment "The Exchange" which opened in 2007. [Penlee House](#), an art gallery and museum notable for its collection of paintings by members of the Newlyn School. The Penzance seafront with its promenade and the open-air seawater [Jubilee Bathing Pool](#) (one of the oldest surviving Art Deco swimming baths in the country). The broad sweeping Promenade beyond gives glorious views out to sea and for many miles along the sweeping coasts of the [Cornish Riviera,](#) with [St Michael's Mount](#) visible away to the left and [Land's End](#) round the corner to the right.

FUN FACT: DID YOU KNOW THAT…..

Royal Mail Ship, usually seen in its abbreviated form RMS, is the ship prefix used for seagoing vessels that carry mail under contract to the British Royal Mail. The designation dates back to 1840. Any vessel designated as "RMS" has the right both to fly the pennant of the Royal Mail when sailing and to include the Royal Mail "crown" insignia with any identifying device and/or design for the ship. It was once commonly used by many shipping lines in the days of ocean liners and channel packets. But today there are just three ships which are designated Royal Mail Ship so it is a very rare designation today.

The three ships are: RMS Scillonian III was built in 1977 and is a ferry operated by the Isles of Scilly Steamship Group between Penzance and the Isles of Scilly. RMS Queen Mary 2 transatlantic ocean liner and cruise ship operated by Cunard Line and built in 2004. She still operates the transatlantic crossing between Southampton and New York between March and October each year as well as cruising. RMS Segwun which is a steamship sailing on the Muskoka Lakes in Ontario in Canada. Built in 1887 she is the oldest operational steamship in North America. She is based at the Muskoka Steamships & Discovery Centre.

https://www.islesofscilly-travel.co.uk/
https://www.cunard.com/en-gb
https://realmuskoka.com/muskoka-steamships/

FUN FACT: DID YOU KNOW THAT…

The first railway-operated bus services in the UK were started by the GWR between Helston railway station and the Lizard on 17 August 1903. On the 31 October 1903 further bus services were introduced between Penzance and Marazion. These were so successful that further routes were introduced from Penzance to St Just and Land's End. Known by the GWR as "road motors", these chocolate-and-cream buses operated throughout the company's territory on railway feeder services and excursions until the early 1930s.

In the early 1930s the railway companies transferred their bus operations either to local bus operators or railway owned bus companies instead of operating them directly. The GWR had its own local bus operators such as:

- **Western National** (founded in 1929 by the GWR for bus services in much of GWR territory in the South West),
- **Devon General** (founded in 1929 jointly by the GWR and the Southern Railway for their bus services in South Devon) and
- **Western Welsh** (founded in 1929 by the GWR for their bus services in much of South and West Wales).
- **Western Transport** (founded in 1930 by the GWR) for their bus services in Mid and North Wales but in 1933 it was merged with LMS's Crosville Motor Services)

The Southern Railway had its own local bus operators including: **Southern National** (founded in 1929 by the SR for their bus services in much of SR territory in Dorset, North Devon and North Cornwall), **Devon General** (jointly founded in 1929 by the GWR and the Southern Railway for their bus operations in South Devon) and **Southern Vectis** (founded in 1929 by the SR for their bus services on the Isle of Wight).

So these GWR bus operations from 1903 became the origin of today's bus network in Cornwall which is operated by Transport for Cornwall, so the legacy of the railways and its pioneering innovations is very long lasting!

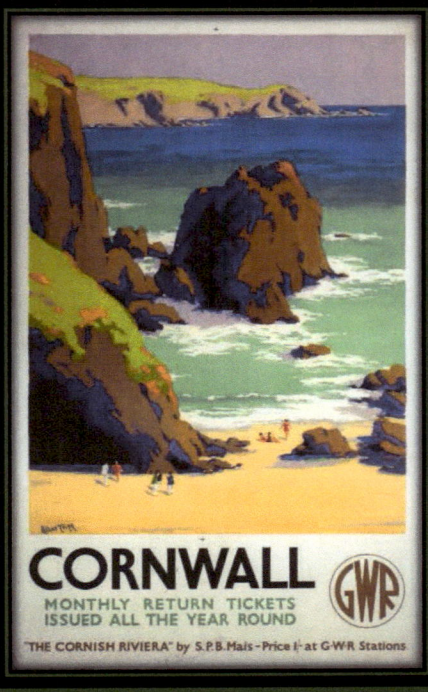

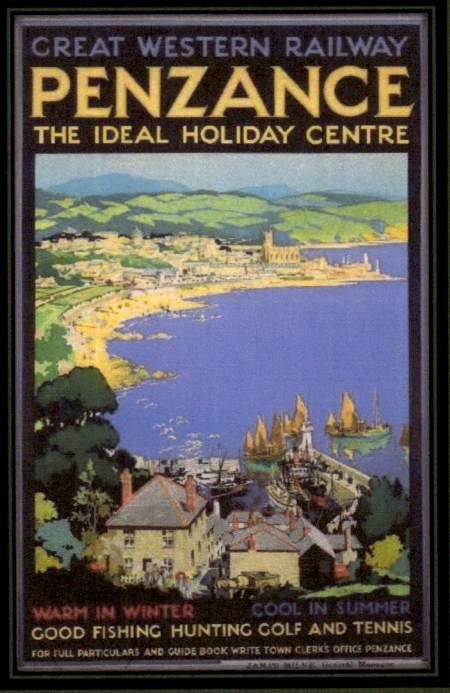

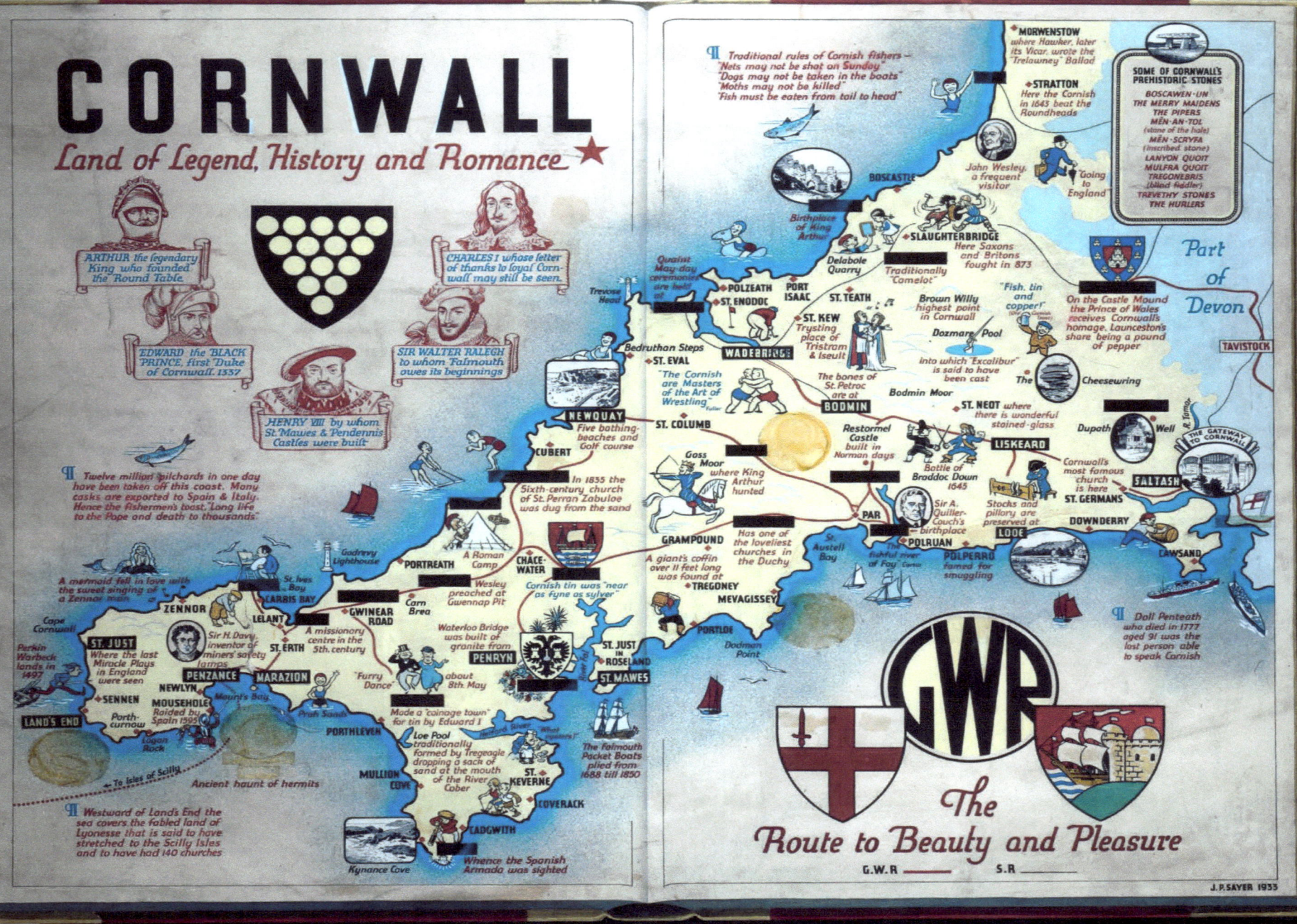

The Night Riviera Sleeper

THE NIGHT RIVIERA SLEEPER

(London Paddington to Penzance)

Introduction:

Sleeper Trains epitomise the romance of travel and have a magic touch and cosmopolitan spirit to them as you go to sleep in one location and wake up refreshed in another. They are convenient, cost effective and environmentally friendly ways to travel. These lifeline trains allow people to make connections – for business, leisure and family – in a way that no other mode of transport can. In recent years, sleeper trains in Britain have experienced a great revival in their fortunes.

Sleeper trains have operated in Britain since Victorian times and offered comfortable overnight accommodation on long distance and some medium distance journeys, allowing passengers to leave their home station in the early and late evening and arrive at the destination at a civilised time the following morning. Often they conveyed restaurant cars, so that dinner could be enjoyed before retiring and, on longer journeys, breakfast in the morning.

The earliest sleeper carriages were introduced in Britain in 1873 by the North British Railway on the Anglo-Scottish route between Edinburgh Waverley and London Kings Cross. The first sleeping car train on the Great Western Railway was introduced at the end of 1877 from London Paddington to Plymouth. An additional service was soon added from London to Penzance which eventually became known as the forerunner of today's Night Riviera Sleeper. The Great Western Railway introduced the familiar sleeping car layout with an internal side corridor and compartments containing berths. This became the British conventional sleeping car, introduced by a variety of railways.

The main sleeper trains services in Britain gradually became focussed on the following:

- London to Scotland (Anglo-Scottish services)
- London and the West Country (Devon and Cornwall)
- London and northern cities.

- London to Paris and Brussels (via train ferry) The Night Ferry

Flagship sleeper services included the following titled trains:

- The Night Scotsman (London Kings Cross to Edinburgh Waverley)
- The Aberdonian (London Kings Cross to Aberdeen)
- The Highlandman (London Kings Cross to Inverness and Fort William)
- The Night Scot (London Euston to Glasgow Central)
- The Royal Highlander (London Euston to Inverness, Aberdeen and Oban)
- The Northern Irishman (London Euston to Stranraer Harbour)
- The Night Riviera (London Paddington to Plymouth and Penzance)
- The Night Ferry (London Victoria to Paris Nord via Dover / Dunkerque train ferry)

In the interwar years a large number of generally quite modern overnight sleeping carriages were inherited by the Big Four railway companies. Yet from the 1920s a great deal of new sleeper carriages were built by the Big Four. The railways decided to build these new sleeper carriages in order to meet increased competition from other modes of transport combined with a greater customer expectation of what should be provided. Sleeping carriages are heavier passenger for passenger, than ordinary stock and their capacity for revenue generation is not as high per ton weight as a conventional day carriage. Also sleeper carriages could only be used once a day so would generate less revenue for the railway compared to day carriages.

However the Big Four railways were surprisingly lavish in the provisions made for sleeper trains which at best were likely to be only marginally profitable and at worst a heavy loss maker. But the reason for this is that they were convinced that passengers will pay due regard to "on train" facilities and amenities when making the fundamental decision whether to use the railways in the first place. So for these reasons the railways continued to build new sleeping carriages. Sleeper trains were always the type of vehicles which gave the railways publicity and status, especially on their more celebrated train services and all of the Big Four made significant steps forward during the interwar period in terms of sleeper carriage design.

In regard to sleeper train services there were really only two significant competitors in the Big Four period and these were the LMS and LNER on the Anglo-Scottish routes. They both became rather good at sleeping cars and set the trend for the first generation British Rail sleeping cars in the 1950s. The traditional British sleeping car layout (side corridor giving access to a series of compartments with berths) never varied during the whole Big Four period. Until 1928 when third class sleeping cars were introduced, there were only first class sleeping cars.

As usual the LMS and LNER on their Anglo-Scottish routes led the way in terms of concept and quantity, producing some very handsome, innovative and well appointed sleeping cars for these services.

Meanwhile the GWR offering initially did not display the innovation of the LMS and LNER carriages. In 1929 the GWR decided to build its own version of the LMS / LNER sleeping cars and they were much more successful. They made full use of the generous GWR loading gauge and were given bulging sides in order to lengthen the berths slightly. They also had recessed end entrance doors, and in these two respects they also set the standard for the GWR during the interwar period. A further batch with more restricted dimensions for cross country work were built in 1934.

British Rail:

After nationalisation in the British Rail era there were two major investments in the sleeper fleet. The first occurred between 1957 and 1964 when 380 Mark 1 carriages were built to replace the fleets inherited from the GWR, LMS and LNER.

In 1966 British Rail launched the **InterCity** brand for its long distance services. From its birth in 1966 the **InterCity** concept quickly caught the public imagination in Britain and started a path that would place it among the world leaders in provision of quality long distance rail transport in the following decades.

British Rail also had car carrying trains which had their origins in the Anglo-Scottish Car Carrier launched in 1955. These services offered sleeper accommodation on a train which also carried the passenger's own cars. The services grew in popularity and a number of loading facilities in London expanded to include Kings Cross, Holloway and Marylebone. There were three kinds of car-

carrying trains operated by British Rail. The CAR-SLEEPER and the CAR-CARRIER service passenger and car travel by the same train. With the CAR-TOURIST service passenger and car travel by separate trains, the car travelling through the night and the passenger by day or night. In the mid 1960s a dedicated station and specialised loading facility in London was created at Kensington Olympia. On 24 May 1966 all the car carrying trains operated by British Rail were relaunched as the **Motorail** network. This was a great success story for British Rail and in the 1970s with frustration about long distance car travel and high petrol prices the services were well patronised for over a decade.

In 1969 the decision was made to market all of Britain's sleeper trains as **InterCity Sleepers**.

In 1973 British Rail created **Travellers Fare** to undertake all its onboard catering. For a while it was linked with **British Transport Hotels**, but when these were privatised in the 1980s, **Travellers Fare** moved to become a division under the control of British Rail. It provided station facilities and on board catering. In June 1986, **InterCity** took over the onboard catering for its services as **InterCity Catering Services**. In December 1986 **Travellers Fare** was privatised.

During this period the list of sleeper trains operated was still very extensive despite some minor withdrawal of services in the 1960s and 70s. By 1975 the BR sleeper train services included the following:

- London Kings Cross to Leeds
- London Kings Cross to Newcastle upon Tyne
- London Kings Cross to Edinburgh, Fort William and Aberdeen.
- London Euston to Liverpool Lime Street
- London Euston to Manchester Piccadilly
- London Euston to Holyhead
- London Euston to Preston and Barrow in Furness
- London Euston to Carlisle and Stranraer Harbour

- London Euston to Glasgow Central and Inverness
- London Paddington to Milford Haven
- London Paddington to Exeter, Plymouth and Penzance
- London Victoria to Paris and Brussels (The Night Ferry)
- Bristol to Glasgow and Edinburgh
- Nottingham to Glasgow

In addition to these, sleepers were provided on a number of **Motorail** services, many of which were seasonal.

In the late 1970s British Rail talked about a major second investment in the sleeping car fleet including options for 75 ft long air conditioned vehicles with improved standards of ride, sound insulation, décor and amenities generally. It was felt that they should be "travelling hotels" with the provision of a bar / refreshment area in each set of three coaches with continental breakfast facilities in all compartments. These aspirations were admirable for the time but were overtaken by major changes in the market for medium and long distance travel and increasing customer expectations for overnight accommodations. These became the Mark III sleeper carriages which were built in Derby by British Rail.

In building the new Mark III sleeper carriages without ensuite facilities, this proved to be a major mistake by British Rail which continued to hinder the Caledonian Sleeper and Night Riviera sleeper services for years. As a result the market for sleeper services declined in the 1980s and 90s. Other important factors that affected the market for sleeper services in this period included the introduction of low cost domestic flights from a number of regional airports which particularly affected the Anglo-Irish traffic via the ferry services. This led to the closure of the sleeper services from London to Stranraer Harbour, Holyhead and Fishguard Harbour that linked with Irish Sea ferry services. Significant modernisation and electrification enabled major journey time reductions on key routes to major cities including London to Liverpool, Manchester, Leeds, Preston, Carlisle, Newcastle upon Tyne and South Wales so their sleeper services were no longer required. The international "Night Ferry" sleeper service from London Victoria to Paris Nord and Brussels via the Dover-Dunkirk train ferry ceased in 1980.

In 1982 **InterCity** sector of British Rail was restructured into a series of route units. The Anglo-Scottish sleeper services were placed in under West Coast route and the London to the West Country sleeper services were under Great Western route.

On 11 July 1983 the London Paddington to Penzance sleeper was relaunched as the **Night Riviera Sleeper**, designed to complement the long-established daytime Cornish Riviera Express.

On 6 May 1987 **InterCity Sleepers** was relaunched with Lounge Cars and Sleeper Check In. By this time the sleeper services were focussed on the Anglo-Scottish services and the Paddington to Penzance service and other services had ceased.

Instead of two competing Anglo-Scottish services via the WCML and ECML it was combined into a single service operating out of London Euston with just two 16-car trains each night, the first to Aberdeen, Inverness and Fort William, and the second to Glasgow Central and Edinburgh Waverley. Lounge cars were introduced serving simple cooked meals and light refreshments. Loss of sleeper services from the ECML caused much public protest as did the loss of the sleeper to Stranraer Harbour.

In 1992 Sleeper and Motorail services were combined to form the **InterCity Overnight Services** business unit. By 1992 **InterCity** reached the height of its success and became an integrated business within British Rail.

InterCity was one of the best known brands in Britain, with an 82% brand awareness which had taken 25 years to develop. It was a well-defined business with a highly successful track record in profit, performance, marking and quality delivery. Sadly the Government decided to split the railways on a route basis and this resulted in the break-up of InterCity as a business and as a brand. Ownership of the **InterCity** brand name transferred to the Department of Transport who continue to own it today. On 31 March 1994 **InterCity** closed as a corporate business within British Rail with a final profit of £100 million.

In 1992 the Government announced plans to privatise the railways in 1994. On the 28 May 1994 **Motorail** services were withdrawn. On 5 March 1995, responsibility for operation of the Anglo-Scottish sleeper services passed within British Rail from InterCity West Coast to ScotRail. On 4 June 1996, the service was relaunched as the **Caledonian Sleeper** with the Night Caledonian (to Glasgow Central), Night Scotsman (to Edinburgh Waverley), Night Aberdonian (to Aberdeen), Royal Highlander (to Inverness) and West Highlander (to Fort William) sub-brands.

Recent Years:

Privatisation in the mid-1990s (1993-1997) also presented another major challenge for overnight sleeper services and resulted in the loss of the Bristol to Glasgow / Edinburgh service. The **Caledonian Sleeper** was placed within the Scotrail franchise and the **Night Riviera Sleeper** was part of the Great Western franchise.

Thus the sleeper train services evolved into the two routes we see today:

- The Caledonian Sleeper (London to Glasgow Central, Edinburgh Waverley, Aberdeen, Inverness and Fort William)
- The Night Riviera Sleeper (London Paddington to Penzance)

Caledonian Sleeper website: https://www.sleeper.scot/

Night Riviera Sleeper website: https://www.gwr.com/travelling-with-us/night-riviera-sleeper

In 2015 the Scottish Government decided to separate the **Caledonian Sleeper** from the Scotrail franchise and placed it in its own dedicated franchise. During 2019, a new fleet of Mark 5 carriages were introduced, replacing the British Rail-era carriages. These are hauled by a combination of Class 92 electric locomotives (on electrified sections only) and rebuilt Class 73/9s electro-diesel locomotives. Today the **Caledonian Sleeper** operates as two main trains from London Euston to destinations in Scotland. These are operated on six days each week (not Saturday night/Sunday morning).

- *The Highland Sleeper* has three portions that serve routes to Aberdeen, Inverness and Fort William.

- *The Lowland Sleeper* has two portions serving routes to Edinburgh Waverley and Glasgow Central.

https://www.youtube.com/watch?v=p4JEStzVQFc

(promotional film about the Caledonian Sleeper from 2020)

https://www.youtube.com/watch?v=YcU90objkkI

(promotional film celebrating the 150th anniversary of Anglo-Scottish sleeper services from 2023)

Meanwhile the **Night Riviera Sleeper** continues to thrive in the Great Western franchise and this was extensively refurbished by 2018. This refit has dramatically enhanced the onboard experience. Today the Night Riviera Sleeper runs six nights a week (Sunday–Friday) between London Paddington and Penzance with one train in each direction.

https://www.youtube.com/watch?v=lV6UHjDPn0g
(promotional film for refurbished Night Riviera sleeper service by Great Western Railway from 2017)

Today the Night Riviera Sleeper is operated by Great Western Railway and usually comprises four or five sleeper coaches (but up to six at peak times) (with night cabins), a restaurant / lounge car and two day coaches (with regular seats).

Typically, the Night Riviera Sleeper usually is ready waiting in Platform 1 at London Paddington by 2100 with passengers able to board at around 2230. The train was refitted in 2018 and this has transformed the experience. All passengers booked in night cabins can enjoy use of First Class Lounges and showers at London Paddington, Truro and Penzance rail stations. The Lounge Car offers light refreshments in the evening and room service is available too. A light breakfast is served to you in your cabin in the morning. Today the Night Riviera Sleeper is very popular and is often fully booked especially in summer.

The Night Riviera is the only way of reaching London from Cornwall before 0900, doing a full day's business and then returning home in comfort. For a region where incomes are far below the national average and house prices are high, this ability for businesses to punch above their weight in London is vital. Therefore the Night Riviera's role in creating and sustaining jobs in Cornwall is out of all proportion to the number of passengers it carries. Indeed it makes a profit and is going from strength to strength. Even though the distance covered is small compared with some sleeper services in Continental Europe, daytime journey times between London and Cornwall remain long. So the Night Riviera is a genuine lifeline service.

The Destinations

The destinations and coastal resorts served by the route and its branches include:

Penzance

It is the most westerly major town in Cornwall and is the terminus of the Cornish Riviera Express from London Paddington. Penzance is perfectly positioned as a gateway to some of Cornwall's most famous tourist destinations, including the Isles of Scilly. It's only a few miles from places such as St Ives, Land's End, and of course St Michael's Mount. Towards the end of the 19th century and into the 20th, the nearby fishing villages of Newlyn, Mousehole and Lamorna became very popular with artists, who are now known as the Newlyn School. They mainly painted outdoor scenes, known commonly as 'en plein air' and over the years have become much sought after. The Penlee House Gallery & Museum in Penzance gives an introduction to the paintings by the Newlyn School of Artists. The nearby sub-tropical Morrab Gardens has a large collection of tender trees and shrubs, many of which cannot be grown outdoors anywhere else in the UK. Also of interest is the seafront with its promenade and the open-air seawater Jubilee Pool (one of the oldest surviving Art Deco swimming baths in the country). Notable hotel in Penzance is the *Queens Hotel*.

https://www.visitcornwall.com/destinations/penzance
https://lovepenzance.co.uk/
https://www.penzancedrydock.com/

FUN FACT: DID YOU KNOW THAT……
In Penzance, down by the harbour is the Dolphin Inn, which is said to have been the first place in Britain where tobacco was smoked. It is also said to have housed Sir John Hawkins during the Spanish Armada campaign and to have been one of the venue used for trials over which Hanging Judge Jeffreys presided in the 17th century during the reign of King James II.

St. Ives

St Ives is accessible by train and is served by a branch line from St Erth on the mainline and is a wonderful coastal resort in Cornwall. St Ives is known for its surf beaches. St Ives has five fantastic beaches to choose from, these range from Porthmeor, with its almost constant surf, to the family friendly Porthminster nestled below the railway station. In-between you have Town Beach, always busy and with every facility near by, and the two east facing beaches, Porthgwidden and the tiny Bamaluz, reached by steep steps below the museum. St Ives is also well known for its art scene. The seafront Tate St Ives gallery has rotating modern art exhibitions, focusing on British artists. Nearby, the Barbara Hepworth Museum and Sculpture Garden, in the modernist artist's former studio, displays her bronzes and other works. People claim St Ives has a light like nowhere else. It has certainly inspired many over the years, from the naïve art of Alfred Wallis to the bold colourful work of Terry Frost, both of whom feature in the exhibitions at Tate St Ives.

Notable hotel in St Ives is the *Tregenna Castle Hotel*.

https://www.visitcornwall.com/destinations/st-ives

https://www.stives-cornwall.co.uk/

https://greatscenicrailways.co.uk/lines/st-ives-bay-line/

FUN FACT: DID YOU KNOW THAT……

Smeaton's Pier is an iconic symbol of St Ives. It must have been painted and photographed more than almost any other pier in the UK. It is far prettier and more interesting than its name suggests! It was named after the pier engineer in charge who was called John Smeaton (who famously designed the third Eddystone Lighthouse which now stands on Plymouth Hoe). It was built between 1767 and 1770 and interestingly has a reservoir at its base. This fills up at high tide, helping to reduce the wave action into the harbour. There are 2 lighthouses on there, the older smaller one is where the pier used to end. It was extended in the 1890s and the larger, white lighthouse was built.

FUN FACT: DID YOU KNOW THAT……

The Sloop Inn is an iconic landmark of St Ives and is rumoured to be the oldest pub in the town dating from 1312.

Falmouth

Falmouth is accessible by train and is served by a branch line from Truro on the mainline and is a wonderful coastal resort in Cornwall. Falmouth is known for its deep natural harbour on the Fal Estuary, and beaches like Swanpool and Gyllyngvase. Falmouth has the world's third largest natural deep-water harbour and is the country's first and last port giving rise to maritime tradition of "Falmouth for Orders". The National Maritime Museum Cornwall has interactive galleries and a flotilla of model boats. Falmouth's maritime legacy and coastal culture is a huge part of its charm boasting world class watersports on its sheltered waters including gig rowing, kayaking, diving and regularly hosting sailing events such as Falmouth Regatta, and the Pendennis Cup. On Pendennis Point, Pendennis Castle is a well-preserved 16th-century fortress built by Henry VIII. The award winning Falmouth Art Gallery (free entry) is one of the leading galleries in the South West and is family friendly too. It has changing displays of some of the best British art with a regular programme of special exhibitions complementing works by luminaries such as Henry Scott-Tuke and Sir Alfred Munnings. To the southwest on the Helford River, Trebah Garden has subtropical plants. Combining a fascinating maritime heritage and modern creativity, Falmouth is building a name for itself as one of the South West's leading cultural and festival destinations. There is also an extensive ferry network "Fal River Cornwall" linking places around the Fal Estuary. Falmouth's beaches include Castle beach, Gyllyngvase beach, Swanpool beach and Maenporth beach. Falmouth is a foodie paradise, tuck into freshly caught seafood from the delicious deli's, food festivals, waterside restaurants, and traditional pubs.

Notable hotels in Falmouth are the *Falmouth Hotel*, the *Royal Duchy Hotel* and the Greenbank Hotel

https://www.visitcornwall.com/destinations/falmouth
https://www.falmouth.co.uk/
https://www.falriver.co.uk/
https://greatscenicrailways.co.uk/lines/maritime-line/
https://www.falmouthharbour.co.uk/

FUN FACT: DID YOU KNOW THAT……

Falmouth is the birthplace of the Wind in the Willows children's book. The charming and, now world famous, children's novel, Wind in the Willows, began its life in Falmouth. In fact, the first two letters which formed the basis of the book were written at the Greenbank Hotel, where Kenneth Grahame stayed as a guest in 1907.

FUN FACT: DID YOU KNOW THAT……

In 1688, the town was named as the Royal Mail Packet Station by King James II. Its role was central to the transport of mail destined for Spain and the Mediterranean as far east as Egypt. By 1763, Falmouth was also the Packet Station for transatlantic mail, from Halifax in North America to Surinam in South America. At its peak, around 30 Packet ships operated from Falmouth Packet Station. These routes evolved into the ocean liner routes of the 20th century with rise of steamships.

FUN FACT: DID YOU KNOW THAT……

The news of Admiral Nelson's death was sent to London from Falmouth. The first messenger was John Richards Lapenotiere, of HMS Pickle, who reached the town on 4 November. He then raced to London bearing the dispatches containing the momentous news of Lord Nelson's victory and death in the Battle of Trafalgar on 21 October 1805.

Website: https://www.thetrafalgarway.org/home

Truro

Truro is accessible by train and is located on the mainline. Today it is the modern capital of Cornwall. As Cornwall's one and only city, Truro radiates a chic, urban charm that's reflected in endless shopping opportunities and some of the best restaurants and bars in the county. Once a Norman castle stood where the present day Crown Court is located and Truro thrived as a port for many years. The prosperity of the late 18th and early 19th continues to this day and can be seen today in the elegant town houses that line the city's streets. The impressive gothic revival Truro Cathedral towers over the town. The Royal Cornwall Museum houses objects that reveal Cornwall's history from prehistoric times through to its industrial triumphs, with an Egyptian mummy thrown in for good measure! The museum runs events for families throughout the year. It's a hidden gem. Nearby there are the wonderful gardens at Trelissick and Tregothan. The latter is famed for being where the first tea was grown in the UK in 1999 to put the 'English into English Tea' and the most British tea in history was first sold in 2005 as the Tregothan Classic Tea blend.

https://www.visitcornwall.com/destinations/truro
https://www.visittruro.org.uk/
https://www.nationaltrust.org.uk/visit/cornwall/trelissick
https://tregothnan.co.uk/

FUN FACT: DID YOU KNOW THAT……

Truro Cathedral is one of the newest in Britain, completed in 1910. Truro Cathedral is one of only three cathedrals in the UK to have three spires. The others are Lichfield Cathedral and St Mary's Episcopal Cathedral in Edinburgh.

Fowey

Fowey was once served by a branch line from Lostwithiel on the mainline, but this closed to passenger services many years ago. Today there is a bus link to Fowey from St Austell rail station and this is the best way to reach this coastal resort.

Set in an Area of Outstanding Natural Beauty, this pretty harbour town is situated on the west side of a deep estuary, where the Fowey River reaches the sea. Yachts tack back and forth across the water while gulls cry overhead. Get an overview of the beautiful harbour with a stroll out along the Esplanade, passing the grand parade of Edwardian and Victorian houses, to the beach at Readymoney Cove overlooked by the medieval St Catherine's Castle guarding the harbour entrance. Across the water, the village of Polruan is said to be far older than Fowey, its medieval blockhouse once housing a chain which could be pulled up to stop boats entering the harbour. As you walk the narrow streets where mediaeval and Georgian buildings cast shadows over each other, a vibrant maritime history of Fowey comes to life. Fowey has been an inspiration for authors for over 100 years. Daphne Du Maurier lived in and around the town and based several of her novels, including 'Rebecca', 'The Loving Spirit' and 'House on the Strand' in the area.

Notable hotels in Fowey are the *Fowey Hotel* (now the [Harbour Hotel Fowey](#)) and the [Fowey Hall Hotel](#).
https://www.visitcornwall.com/destinations/fowey

FUN FACT: DID YOU KNOW THAT……

Fowey was the main port for loading ammunition for the US 29th Division that landed on Omaha Beach on D-Day during the Second World War. There was a munitions railway siding at Woodgate Pill just north of Fowey, originally built for the First World War. The D-Day Landings were the largest seaborne invasion in history. The operation began the liberation of France, and the rest of Western Europe, and laid the foundations of the Allied victory on the Western Front.

Newquay

Newquay is accessible by train and is served by a branch line from Par on the mainline and is a wonderful coastal resort in Cornwall. Perched on Cornwall's Atlantic Coast and bordered by several miles of golden beaches, it's no wonder Newquay is one of the nation's favourite seaside towns. Recent years have seen Newquay blossom as a destination for lovers of good food, with restaurants such as Rick Steins' Fistral taking advantage of the beachside views and fresh-caught fish to serve a classic seaside meal whilst watching the surf. Newquay is also the surfing capital of Britain with its world famous Fistral Beach. Newquay's already lively atmosphere is given a huge boost by its annual festivals and events, the biggest probably being the Boardmasters Festival, a combination of surfing and music that attracts not only some of the world's best surfers, but also top bands and singers from across the globe. Away from that, there are fish festivals, beer festivals, open air theatre and a host of other events packed into the year.

Notable hotels in Newquay are the [Headland Hotel](), the [Atlantic Hotel Newquay](), the [Great Western Hotel](), the [Harbour Hotel Newquay]() and the [Fistral Beach Hotel]().
https://www.visitcornwall.com/destinations/newquay
https://www.visitnewquay.org/
https://greatscenicrailways.co.uk/lines/atlantic-coast-line/

FUN FACT: DID YOU KNOW THAT……

The legendary Beatles band filmed the Magical Mystery Tour TV film in 1967 partly at the Atlantic Hotel, and on Towan Beach in Newquay. It is the third film that starred the band and depicts a group of people on a coach tour who experience strange happenings caused by magicians. The film originally aired on BBC1, in black-and-white, on Boxing Day, 26 December 1967. A colour transmission followed on BBC2 on 5 January 1968.

Looe

Looe is accessible by train and is served by a branch line from Liskeard on the mainline and is a wonderful coastal resort in Cornwall. Looe's main beach at East Looe offers soft golden sand and slopes gently to provide safe swimming and a regular sun trap. It is easily accessible from the town providing all you need for a relaxing day including cafes and shops. Bordered by the unique Banjo Pier, visitors have been enjoying the beach and its bathing waters for over 200 years. Once a holy pilgrimage site, Looe Island, which sits just off the seafront at West Looe, is now a sanctuary for rare plants and wildlife. Left to the Cornwall Wildlife Trust in 2004 by the Atkins sisters who had lived and owned the island since the mid-1960s, the trust has continued to manage the island as a nature reserve ever since. They allow visitors to explore the island throughout the summer via boat trips from the harbour at Looe. The island is home to many nesting birds such as cormorants, shags and oystercatchers. It has the largest breeding colony in Cornwall of the majestic great black-backed gull. On the rocks and in the waters around the island, grey seals can often be seen in the summer months. With adult males weighing over 200 kg, they are Britain's largest mammal and although common in the seas around Cornwall, are quite rare elsewhere in the UK. Looe's harbour and river separates east from west and is spanned by a Victorian bridge. Surrounded by hotels and restaurants, it's the ever changing focal point of the town as the tide goes in and out, boats come and go and there's a constant flow of people going about their daily life.

https://www.visitcornwall.com/destinations/looe

https://www.visitlooe.co.uk/

https://greatscenicrailways.co.uk/lines/looe-valley-line/

https://greatscenicrailways.co.uk/looe-rail-heritage/

FUN FACT: DID YOU KNOW THAT……

Off the coast from Looe is located Looe Island. This island itself has an amazing history as it dates back to prehistoric times and there have been many owners, including the Trelawny family. Sir Jonathan Trelawny was Bishop of Bristol, Exeter and Winchester, one of the Seven Bishops tried under King James II in 1628, and the hero of the Cornish ballad 'The Song of the Western Men' known for the refrain 'and shall Trelawny die' written by R.S. Hawker. Today the island is a nature reserve owned by the Cornish Wildlife Trust.

FUN FACT: DID YOU KNOW THAT……

For over 300 years, the coastlines of the English Channel and south west of England were at the mercy of Barbary pirates (corsairs) from North Africa. They were based out of the ports of Algiers, Tunis and Tripoli. The fishing ports of Cornwall including Looe were a particular target in the 17th century and many young men were kidnapped and ransomed or sold as slaves in the Arab slave markets. Sometimes their wives and children were also targeted. By the 1650s it was thought that there were thousands of English people held captive by the Barbary pirates in Algiers. This caused significant disruption to the Cornish fishing industry with people being reluctant to put to sea out of fear of being kidnapped or leaving their families unprotected on shore. The piracy menace was finally ended in 1816 following an attack by the British and Dutch navies which broke the power of the pirates forever and liberated their captives.

Padstow

Historically Padstow wasn't served by train on the GWR's Cornish Riviera Express route from London Paddington, but instead by its arch rival which was the Southern Railway's Atlantic Coast Express from London Waterloo! Indeed it was the western terminus of the famed Atlantic Coast Express. Today sadly it has lost its rail link and is now there is a bus link to Bodmin, Wadebridge and Padstow from Bodmin Parkway rail station and this is the best way to reach this coastal resort.

Made famous by Rick Stein over the last 30 years or so, there's much more to Padstow than just great places to eat. It's still a working harbour, it's surrounded by glorious beaches, and offers a base to explore the Camel estuary. Enjoy a fun filled day out on one of the many beaches in the Padstow area. If you want golden sand, this is the place to come, from the tidal beaches at Hawker's Cove to the long strands at Harlyn and Treyarnon. Hop on the ferry and explore Rock or Daymer Bay or take the surf boards to Constantine Bay. The mouth of the Camel Estuary is known and feared by many seafarers for the notorious Doom Bar. This is a sandbar that can move depending on the currents, especially after storms. Until the 20th Century, access to the safety of the estuary was under the cliffs of Stepper Point, but this could mean loss of wind for the sailing ships of the time, and many were lost in gales. In the early 20th century, the bar shifted considerably but with continuous dredging a safe channel has been created, but it can still catch some sailors out.

Notable hotel in Padstow is the *Metropole Hotel (now the Harbour Hotel Padstow)*.

https://www.visitcornwall.com/destinations/padstow

https://padstowlive.com/

https://padstow-harbour.co.uk/

FUN FACT: DID YOU KNOW THAT……

Possibly from as early as 2,500 BC Padstow has been used as a natural harbour linking Brittany to Ireland along the 'Saints Way' from Fowey on the south coast of Cornwall. Legend has it that St Petroc possibly one of the most important of the Cornish Saints arrived from Ireland around 520 AD and built a monastery on the hill above the harbour. In medieval times the port grew and trade with Ireland and Brittany developed as well as coastal trade with South Wales. Today Padstow remains the only sizeable estuary on the north coast of Cornwall and so remains an important community.

FUN FACT: DID YOU KNOW THAT……

Padstow is home to the Doom Bar, a treacherous sandbank that has been the cause of more than 600 shipwrecks in 200 years. It is said that the Doom Bar is the result of a mermaid who watched over the vessels that went in and out of Padstow. One day, she was shot by a sailor on a visiting boat. Her curse was that the harbour would become desolate from that time on. Today there is a beer named the Doom Bar which is brewed by Sharp's Brewery in Rock across from Padstow. Doom Bar is the UK's best selling cask and bottled ale, born on the North Cornish coast. Doom Bar is a perfectly balanced beer combining subtle yet complex flavours. This creates an amber ale which is both satisfying and deliciously moreish

The Lizard

The Lizard is famed as the most southerly point of the British mainland. The Lizard's coast is particularly hazardous to shipping and the seaways round the peninsula were historically known as the "Graveyard of Ships". The Lizard Lighthouse was built at Lizard Point in 1752 and the RNLI operates The Lizard lifeboat station. The Lizard Lighthouse was automated by Trinity House and the lighthouse keepers departed in 1998. Its light was often the welcoming beacon to persons returning to England, where on a clear night, the reflected light could be seen 100 miles (160 km) away across the ocean. Its deafening foghorn could be heard over 20 miles away. The lighthouse foghorns around the UK were a historic part of the soundscape of the coast with their deafening roars and bellows each unique to the location, along with the myriad of ship's whistles and foghorns as vessels made their way along the coast. On 13 July 2009 HRH The Princess Royal officially opened the Lizard Lighthouse Heritage Centre telling the story of the lighthouse and role of Trinity House in navigation safety. In modern times, the Lizard Lighthouse forms one point of an important protective triangle – Longships Lighthouse (at Land's End), Wolf Rock Lighthouse and the Lizard Lighthouse collectively create one of the most well lit waterways in the British Isles.

The Lizard also has a historically important role in the story of telecommunications. In 1900 Guglielmo Marconi stayed the Housel Bay Hotel in his quest to locate a coastal radio station to receive signals from ships equipped with his apparatus. He leased a plot "in the wheat field adjoining the hotel" where the Lizard Wireless Telegraph Station still stands today. Recently restored by the National Trust, it looks as it did in January 1901, when Marconi received the distance record signals of 186 miles (299 km) from his transmitter station at Niton, Isle of Wight.

Today the Lizard Wireless Station is the oldest Marconi station to survive in its original state, and is located to the west of the Lloyds Signal Station in what appears to be a wooden hut. On 12 December 1901 Poldhu Point was the site of the very first transatlantic, wireless signal radio communication when Marconi sent a signal to St John's, Newfoundland. The technology is one of the key advances to the development of radio, television, satellites and the internet.

The Goonhilly Earth Station is located on the Lizard and also played a historic role in the story of telecommunications particularly in regard to tracking satellites. It was once the largest satellite earth station in the world, with more than 30 communication antennas and dishes in use. The site also links into undersea cable lines. Its first satellite dish, Antenna One (dubbed "Arthur"), was built in 1962 to link with Telstar. It was the first open parabolic design and is 25.9 metres (85 feet) in diameter and weighs 1,118 tonnes. After Pleumeur-Bodou Ground Station (Brittany) which received the first live transatlantic television broadcasts from the United States via the Telstar satellite at 0H47 GMT on 11 July 1962, "Arthur" received his first video in the middle of the same day. It is now a Grade II listed structure and is therefore protected. The site has also played a key role in broadcasting major world events such as the Muhammad Ali fights, the Apollo 11 Moon Landing in 1969, and 1985's Live Aid concert. The site's largest dish, dubbed "Merlin", has a diameter of 32 metres (105 feet). Other dishes include Guinevere, Tristan, and Isolde after characters in Arthurian legend, much of which takes place in Cornwall.

On the Lizard Peninsular there is also RNAS Culdrose which is Europe's largest helicopter base, and currently hosts the Training and Operational Conversion Unit operating the EH101 "Merlin" helicopter. It is also the home base for Merlin Squadrons embarked upon Royal Navy warships, the Westland Sea King airborne early warning (AEW) variant helicopter, a Search And Rescue (Sea King, again) helicopter flight, and some BAe Hawk T.1 trainer jets used for training purposes by the Royal Navy. The base also operates some other types of fixed wing aircraft for calibration and other training purposes. As befits the base's name, a non-flying example of a Hawker Sea Hawk forms the main gate guardian static display. RNAS Culdrose is a major contributor to the economy of The Lizard area.

It can be a beautiful place, but it can also be a wild place. For hundreds of years, it has been the first sighting of land for sailors heading home from foreign shores and it's often a place of refuge for rare birds blown off course when out at sea."

Notable hotel at the Lizard is the *Housel Bay Hotel*.

https://www.visitcornwall.com/regions/the-lizard

https://www.trinityhouse.co.uk/lighthouses-and-lightvessels/lizard-lighthouse

https://www.nationaltrust.org.uk/visit/cornwall/lizard-point

Goonhilly Earth Station Ltd

https://www.royalnavy.mod.uk/our-organisation/bases-and-stations/air-stations/rnas-culdrose

Land's End

Land's End is the legendary Cornish destination that has inspired people for centuries and is famed as the most western point of the English mainland. Land's End has a particular resonance because it is often used to suggest distance. Land's End to John o' Groats in Scotland is a distance of 838 miles (1,349 km) by road and this Land's End to John o' Groats distance is often used to define charitable events such as end-to-end walks and races in the UK. Throughout the ages, Land's End has held a fascination for many people and the place has inspired many stories and works of art. The mythical 'Lost Land of Lyonesse' is said to lie beneath the waves between Land's End and the Isles of Scilly. There are over 130 recorded shipwrecks around Land's End and it has long been a risk to shipping with its rocky outcrops and jagged rocks proving tricky to navigate. In modern times, Longships Lighthouse at Land's End forms one point of an important protective triangle – Longships Lighthouse, Wolf Rock Lighthouse and the Lizard Lighthouse collectively create one of the most well lit waterways in the British Isles.

Notable hotel at Land's End is the famed [Land's End Hotel](https://landsend-landmark.co.uk/).
https://landsend-landmark.co.uk/

FUN FACT: DID YOU KNOW THAT……

Land's End will forever be synonymous with its furthest British neighbour, John O'Groats in the far north of Scotland. Every year, people make the journey which takes 14 hours by car or up to three months on foot! The End to End story is a fascinating exhibit at the visitor attraction, celebrating the stories of people who have completed this 800-mile challenge.

Cornwall's WALKING TRAILS

Cornwall's Walking Trails

As well as its wonderful towns and coastal resorts, Cornwall is crisscrossed by many interesting walking trails. Here we showcase some of the notable walking trails that can be enjoyed across this beautiful county and royal duchy.

The South West Coast Path National Trail:

The longest of England's National Trails, the multi award-winning South West Coast Path offers 630 miles of stunning coastal walking around the entire South West peninsula. Starting at Minehead in Somerset it runs along the coastline of Exmoor, continuing along the coast of North Devon into Cornwall. It follows the entire coastline of Cornwall from Bude to Land's End and across the mouth of the River Tamar to Plymouth. From Plymouth it then continues along the south coast of Devon and it then follows the Dorset coastline before finally ending at Poole Harbour.

https://www.nationaltrail.co.uk/en_GB/trails/south-west-coast-path/

https://www.southwestcoastpath.org.uk/

The Tamara Coast to Coast Way:

In 2023 a new 87 mile walking route that connects the south and north coasts of the South West was opened. The Tamara Coast to Coast Way follows much of the River Tamar and the boundary between Devon and Cornwall. Tamar Valley National Landscape created the route to encourage more people to enjoy this overlooked area. The route traces the course of the River Tamar from the vibrant city of Plymouth to the very source of the Tamar River near Bude.

https://www.tamarvalley-nl.org.uk/discover-explore/walking/tamara-coast-to-coast-way/

The Cornish Way:

The Cornish Way provides a total of 180 miles for walkers and cyclists to explore Cornwall. It runs from Land's End to Bude. The route splits at Truro, with one route going via Padstow and the other via St Austell before joining again at Bodmin.

https://www.cornwall.gov.uk/environment/countryside/cycle-routes-and-trails/

The Camel Trail:

The Camel Trail is an 18 mile largely traffic free, surfaced and virtually level multi use trail centred around the beautiful Camel Estuary as it reaches Padstow. It provides access to the beautiful Cornish countryside along a disused railway line between Wenfordbridge, Bodmin, Wadebridge and Padstow. The section between Wadebridge and Padstow follows the River Camel estuary and is a particularly scenic and beautiful area. It falls into three main sections:

Padstow to Wadebridge - 5.5 Miles

Wadebridge to Bodmin (Boscarne) - 5.75 Miles

Bodmin to Wenfordbridge - 6.25 Miles

https://cameltrail.co.uk/

https://www.cornwall.gov.uk/environment/countryside/cycle-routes-and-trails/the-camel-trail/

The Saint's Way:

The Saints' Way trail crosses mid-Cornwall from coast to coast. It covers approximately 30 miles from the northern harbour town of Padstow to the southern port of Fowey. The route starts at Padstow and heads south through Little Petherick, St Breock Downs and Lanivet. The trail then joins the Fowey River near Lostwithiel and then follows the river to reach Fowey. It traces one of the ancient routes taken by pilgrims, missionaries and travellers from Ireland and Wales who went by sea to Padstow and then overland across Cornwall to Fowey to continue by sea to Mont St Michel in Brittany (France) or to Santiago de Compostela in Galicia (Spain) where the Cathedral of St James is located. This overland journey across Cornwall enabled those from Ireland and Wales travelling to France and Spain to avoid the treacherous waters around Land's End.

https://www.cornwall.gov.uk/environment/countryside/cycle-routes-and-trails/the-saints-trail/

The St Michael's Way:

The St Michael's Way trail runs from coast to coast across Cornwall and stretches from Lelant (near St. Ives) to Marazion (near Penzance) and stretches 12.5 miles. It traces the one of the ancient routes taken by pilgrims, missionaries and travellers from Ireland and Wales who went by sea to St Ives and then overland across Cornwall to Marazion and St Michael's Mount to continue by sea to Mont St Michel in Brittany (France) or to Santiago de Compostela in Galicia (Spain) where the Cathedral of St James is located. This overland journey across Cornwall enabled those from Ireland and Wales travelling to France and Spain to avoid the treacherous waters around Land's End.

https://www.cornwall.gov.uk/environment/countryside/cycle-routes-and-trails/st-michaels-way/

References:

"Through the Window: The Great Western Railway from London Paddington to Penzance", GWR, 1924

"Through the Window: London Paddington to Birkenhead", GWR, 1925

"Through the Window: London Paddington to Killarney via Fishguard and Rosslare", GWR, 1926

"South East England by Train", Paul Atterbury, 1991

"The Golden Age of the Great Western Railway 1895-1914", Tim Bryan, 1991

"The Great Days of the GWR", David St John Thomas and Patrick Whitehouse, 1991

"Readers Digest Touring Guide to Britain", The Readers Digest, 1992

"The History of British Railway Carriages 1900-1953", David Jenkinson, 1996

"The Great Western Railway 150 Glorious Years", Patrick Whitehouse and David St John Thomas, 2002

"Great Scenic Railways of Devon and Cornwall", Michael Pearson, 2004

"Britain from the Rails", Benedict le Vay, 2009

"Mile by Mile on Britain's Railways", S.N. Pike, 2011

"The Encyclopaedia of Titled Trains", Nick Pigott, 2012

"The Intercity Story 1964-2012", Chris Green and Mike Vincent, 2013

"Night Trains - The Rise and Fall of the Sleeper", Andrew Martin, 2017

Image Information:

p3
Photo: Painting by Peter Morath of GWR No 6000 King George V passing Reading West with the Cornish Riviera Express in 1930.
(c) National Railway Museum / Science Museum Group

p4
Photo: GWR "Speed to the West" vintage travel poster 1939. Artwork by Charles Mayo.
(c) National Railway Museum / Science Museum Group

p5 Photo Montage:
Top Left: GWR No 6008 King James II speeds past Twyford on the down Cornish Riviera Express on 3 May 1958.
(c) Colour Rail Archive
Top Right: GWR No 5028 Llantilio Castle awaits departure from Penzance with the up Cornish Riviera Express in Sep 1959.
(c) Colour Rail Archive
Bottom Left: BR Warship class 41 diesel D601 Ark Royal on the Cornish Riviera Express at Dainton ascending the South Devon Banks on 19 June 1958. Notably it was this locomotive that had been the first diesel locomotive to haul the nonstop section of the Cornish Riviera Express from London Paddington to Plymouth on 16 June 1958. (c) Colour Rail Archive
Bottom Right: BR Warship class 42 diesel on the Cornish Riviera Express at Dawlish in 1961.
(c) Colour Rail Archive

p6
Photo: GWR Hitachi Class 802 IEP train enters Cornwall with the Devonport naval base in the background.
(c) Great Western Railway (GWR)

p15
Photo: Overall view of London Paddington looking towards "The Lawn" concourse.
(c) Author's Collection (6 May 2019)

p16 Photo Montage:
Top Left: Modern GWR with three Hitachi IEP trains lined up at the buffer stops at London Paddington.
(c) Author's Collection (6 May 2019)
Top Right: Statue of Isambard Kingdom Brunel on Platforms 8/9 at London Paddington.
(c) Author's Collection (6 May 2019)
Bottom Left: Statue of Paddington Bear on Platform 1 at London Paddington.
(c) Author's Collection (6 May 2019)
Bottom Right: General view along Platform 1 at London Paddington as a Hitachi IEP train awaits departure.
(c) Author's Collection (6 May 2019)

p18
Photo: General view of the Elizabeth Line platforms under London Paddington.
(c) Network Rail

p22
Photo: General view of the new station entrance at Reading following its recent rebuilding work.
(c) Network Rail

p27
Photo: View of the Westbury White Horse from the carriage window of an Intercity 125 HST.
(c) Author's Collection (6 Aug 2018)

p33:
Photo: The Castle Hotel in Taunton.
(c) Author's Collection (5 April 2015)

p34
Photo: The Museum of Somerset in Taunton.
(c) Author's Collection (5 April 2015)

p37
Photo: GWR No 3440 City of Truro rests by the Coaling Stage at Didcot Railway Centre.
(c) Author's Collection (6 May 2007)

p40
Photo: View of the Exeter Ship Canal as people enjoy the evening sunlight.
(c) Author's Collection (27 Aug 2006)

p41
Photo: Exeter Cathedral.
(c) Author's Collection (27 Aug 2006)

p42
Photo: View from the carriage window of Exeter Cathedral over the roofs of houses.
(c) Author's Collection (1 Aug 2020)

p45
Photo: Famed "GWR - 100 Years of Progress" vintage travel poster 1935 showing GWR King class No 6009 King Charles II on an express train at Dawlish near Parson's Tunnel. Artwork by Murray Secretan.
(c) National Railway Museum / Science Museum Group

p46 Photo Montage:
Top Left: View from the carriage window at Dawlish on the famous Brunel Sea Wall section.
(c) Author's Collection (27 July 2019)
Top Right: View along the railway line at Dawlish on the famous Sea Wall section.
(c) Author's Collection (21 Aug 2007)
Bottom Left: View west from the platform at Dawlish station.
(c) Author's Collection (21 Aug 2007)
Bottom Right: Dawlish station
(c) Author's Collection (21 Aug 2007)

p47
Photo: A GWR Hitachi IEP Train rounds the curve at Teignmouth to join the famous Sea Wall section.
(c) Great Western Railway (GWR)

p49 Photo Montage:
Top Left: General view of Newton Abbot rail station.
(c) Author's Collection (29 Aug 2009)
Top Right: Main entrance building at Newton Abbot rail station.
(c) Author's Collection (29 Aug 2009)
Bottom Left: Platform view at Newton Abbot station looking towards London.
(c) Author's Collection (29 Aug 2009)
Bottom Right: BR Intercity 125 HST arrives at Newton Abbot with a train bound for London.
(c) Author's Collection (29 Aug 2009)

p53
Photo: Main entrance and tower block at Plymouth North Road rail station.
(c) Author's Collection (28 Aug 2006)

p55
Photo: View over Plymouth Hoe towards the expanse of Plymouth Sound.
(c) Author's Collection (3 Aug 2015)

p57 Photo Montage:
Top Left: Duke of Cornwall Hotel at Plymouth Millbay Docks.
(c) Author's Collection (3 Aug 2015)
Top Right: Royal Citadel at Plymouth Hoe on the waterfront in Plymouth.
(c) Author's Collection (2 Aug 2015)
Bottom Left: Plymouth Hoe with Smeaton's Tower and the Tinside Lido in Plymouth.
(c) Author's Collection (2 Aug 2015)
Bottom Right: Royal William Yard in Plymouth.
(c) Author's Collection (2 Aug 2015)

p65
Photo: BR(WR) "Royal Albert Bridge - Centenary" vintage travel poster by Terence Cuneo 1958.
(c) National Railway Museum / Science Museum Group

p66
Photo: GWR No 5020 Trematon Castle on the up Cornish Riviera Express crosses the Royal Albert Bridge at Saltash bound for London in April 1959. (c) Colour Rail Archive

p67
Photo: BR Warship class diesel No 600 Active crosses the Royal Albert Bridge at Saltash with the Cornish Riviera Express in 1958.
(c) National Railway Museum / Science Museum Group

p68
Photo: View from the carriage window of a BR Intercity 125 HST as it crosses the Royal Albert Bridge at Saltash.
(c) Author's Collection (6 Aug 2018)

p68 Photo Montage:
Top Left: View from the train of the mighty River Tamar as it crosses the Royal Albert Bridge.
(c) Author's Collection (3 July 2021)
Top Right: View of the train of the River Tamar as it crosses the Royal Albert Bridge.
(c) Author's Collection (3 July 2021)
Bottom Left: View over Saltash from the train as it crosses the Royal Albert Bridge into Cornwall.
(c) Author's Collection (3 July 2021)
Bottom Right: View back towards the River Tamar as the train comes off the Royal Albert Bridge into Cornwall.
(c) Author's Collection (3 July 2021)

P69
Photo: GWR Hitachi Class 802 IEP Train enters Cornwall with the Royal Albert Bridge in the background.
(c) Great Western Railway (GWR)

p71
Photo: View of the Lynher River in Cornwall with the former HMS Brecon moored as a training ship for the HMS Raleigh shore training establishment of the Royal Navy.
(c) Author's Collection (1 Aug 2020)

p73 Photo Montage:
Top Left: Liskeard rail station - main platforms.
(c) Author's Collection (1 Aug 2018)
Top Right: Liskeard rail station - platform for the Looe branch line which is at right angles to the main platforms.
(c) Author's Collection (1 Aug 2018)
Bottom Left: Liskeard rail station - signal box.
(c) Author's Collection (1 Aug 2018)
Bottom Right: Liskeard rail station - main platforms.
(c) Author's Collection (1 Aug 2018)

p76
Photo: Bodmin Parkway rail station.
(c) Author's Collection (5 Aug 2011)

p77
Photo: Steam train on the Bodmin Railway departs Bodmin Parkway bound for Bodmin General.
(c) Author's Collection (5 Aug 2018)

p78 Photo Montage:
Top Left: Main Gatehouse at Lanhydrock House near Bodmin Parkway in Cornwall.
(c) Author's Collection (5 Aug 2018)
Top Right: Lanhydrock House near Bodmin Parkway in Cornwall.
(c) Author's Collection (5 Aug 2018)
Bottom Left: Estate Office at Lanhydrock House.
(c) Author's Collection (5 Aug 2018)
Bottom Right: Bedroom at Lanhydrock House.
(c) Author's Collection (5 Aug 2018)

P79
Photo: GWR Hitachi IEP Train enters Lostwithiel rail station.
(c) Great Western Railway (GWR)

p80
Photo: General view of St Austell rail station.
(c) Author's Collection (1 Aug 2019)

p82
Photo: The Eden Project.
(c) Author's Collection (31 July 2019)

p84
Photo: View of Truro Cathedral from the train.
(c) Author's Collection (29 July 2017)

p89
Photo: St Michael's Mount near Penzance.
(c) Author's Collection (27 July 2022)

p90
Photo: General view of Penzance rail station and the townscape of Penzance and its harbour.
(c) Author's Collection (29 July 2022)

p91
Photo: Penzance rail station with the RMS Scillonian III in the background.
(c) Author's Collection (29 July 2022)

p93
Photo: GWR Cornwall Map vintage travel poster
(c) National Railway Museum / Science Museum Group

p103
Photo: The Night Riviera Sleeper awaits departure from Platform 1 at London Paddington.
(c) Great Western Railway (GWR)

p104 Photo Montage:
Top Left: The Lounge Car on board the Night Riviera Sleeper.
(c) Great Western Railway (GWR)
Top Right: The seating carriage on board the Night Riviera Sleeper.
(c) Great Western Railway (GWR)
Bottom Left: A cabin on board the Night Riviera Sleeper in night mode.
(c) Great Western Railway (GWR)
Bottom Right: A cabin on board the Night Riviera Sleeper in day mode.
(c) Great Western Railway (GWR)

p107
Photo: General view of Penzance.
(c) Author's Collection (27 July 2022)

p108 Photo Montage:
Top Left: Penzance Harbour
(c) Author's Collection (24 July 2022)
Top Right: Penzance Drydocks shipyard.
(c) Author's Collection (24 July 2022)
Bottom Left: Penzance Harbour with the RMS Scillonian III.
(c) Author's Collection (25 July 2022)
Bottom Right: The art deco Jubilee Pool in Penzance.
(c) Author's Collection (29 July 2022)

p109 Photo Montage:
Top Left: View of Penzance station from under the overall roof at the buffer stops with a London train waiting to depart formed of a GWR Hitachi IEP train.
(c) Author's Collection (24 July 2022)
Top Right: General view of Penzance station with the town and the RMS Scillonian III in the background. To the left can be seen the Night Riviera Sleeper and on the right is a London train formed of a GWR Hitachi IEP train.
(c) Author's Collection (24 July 2022)
Bottom Left: Another view of Penzance station with three trains visible including the Night Riviera Sleeper, a local train and the London train formed of a GWR Hitachi IEP train. In the background is RMS Scillonian III awaiting her next sailing to the Isles of Scilly. (c) Author's Collection (24 July 2022)
Bottom Right: External view of Penzance station and its station building.
(c) Author's Collection (27 July 2022)

p110
Photo: Newlyn Harbour near Penzance.
(c) Author's Collection (24 July 2022)

p111
Photo: Atmospheric and moody view of St Michael's Mount and Mount's Bay from Penzance.
(c) Author's Collection (24 July 2022)

p114 Photo Montage:
Top Left: View towards St Ives Harbour from the Malakoff.
(c) Author's Collection (29 July 2022)
Top Right: View of St Ives station from the Malakoff.
(c) Author's Collection (29 July 2022)
Bottom Left: Porthminster Beach in St Ives
(c) Author's Collection (29 July 2022)
Bottom Right: View from the train as you arrive at St Ives showing Porthminster Beach and the Harbour.
(c) Author's Collection (30 July 2017)

p115 Photo Montage:
Top Left: Porthgwidden Beach at St Ives.
(c) Author's Collection (29 July 2022)
Top Right: Porthgwidden Beach at St Ives looking across St Ives Bay.
(c) Author's Collection (29 July 2022)
Bottom Left: The bus station at the Malakoff in St Ives.
(c) Author's Collection (29 July 2022)
Bottom Right: Porthmeor Beach in St Ives near the Tate St Ives.
(c) Author's Collection (30 July 2017)

p116
Photo: General view of St Ives from the Harbour.
(c) Author's Collection (29 July 2022)

p119 Photo Montage:
Top Left: The Falmouth Hotel in Falmouth.
(c) Author's Collection (4 July 2021)
Top Right: View across Falmouth towards the A&P Falmouth shipyard and Pendennis Shipyard with the Spirit of Discovery cruise ship berthed near the National Maritime Museum Cornwall.
(c) Author's Collection (6 July 2021)
Bottom Left: The Prince of Wales Pier in Falmouth where all the Fal River Cornwall ferry services go from.
(c) Author's Collection (6 July 2021)
Bottom Right: View across Falmouth towards the Greenbank Hotel.
(c) Author's Collection (6 July 2021)

p120 Photo Montage:
Top Left: View across Falmouth towards the Greenbank Hotel from Prince of Wales Pier.
(c) Author's Collection (4 July 2021)
Top Right: View across Falmouth to the shipyards.
(c) Author's Collection (4 July 2021)
Bottom Left: The National Maritime Museum Cornwall in Falmouth.
(c) Author's Collection (4 July 2021)
Bottom Right: View across Falmouth Bay from near the Falmouth Hotel.
(c) Author's Collection (4 July 2021)

p121 Photo Montage:
Top Left: St Mawes Harbour with the St Mawes Ferry to Falmouth at its berth.
(c) Author's Collection (8 July 2021)
Top Right: General view of St Mawes as the St Mawes Ferry departs on its way across to Falmouth.
(c) Author's Collection (8 July 2021)
Bottom Left: View of the St Mawes Ferry heading across from St Mawes to Falmouth as it passes St Anthony Lighthouse.
(c) Author's Collection (8 July 2021)
Bottom Right: View of the St Mawes Ferry as it heads across Carrick Roads on its way to Falmouth with Pendennis Castle high on its headland.
(c) Author's Collection (8 July 2021)

p122
Photo: St Mawes Castle looking out across Carrick Roads towards Falmouth Bay as the St Mawes Ferry passes on its way between St Mawes and Falmouth.
(c) Author's Collection (8 July 2021)

p125
Photo: View from Fowey across the River Fowey to Polruan.
(c) Author's Collection (2 Aug 2019)

p126 Photo Montage:
Top Left: The centre of Fowey with the King of Prussia pub.
(c) Author's Collection (2 Aug 2019)
Top Right: View across to Polruan opposite Fowey.
(c) Author's Collection (2 Aug 2019)
Bottom Left: View up the River Fowey from Fowey.
(c) Author's Collection (2 Aug 2019)
Bottom Right: The lane that leads from the bus terminus (outside the Safe Harbour Inn) to the church and the Fowey town centre.
(c) Author's Collection (2 Aug 2019)

p127 Photo Montage:
Left: The Fowey Hotel in Fowey (now the Harbour Hotel Fowey).
(c) Author's Collection (29 July 2019)
Top Right: View across to Polruan from outside the Fowey Hotel in Fowey.
(c) Author's Collection (29 July 2019)
Bottom Right: View across to Fowey from Polruan.
(c) Author's Collection (29 July 2019)

p128 Photo Montage:
These two photos show the lovely narrow lanes of Polruan.
(c) Author's Collection (29 July 2019)

p130
Photo: Fantastic view of Newquay from the Great Western Hotel across Great Western Beach towards Newquay Harbour, the Atlantic Hotel and Towan Head.
(c) Author's Collection (28 July 2019)

p131 Photo Montage:
Top Left: View from near Fistral Beach towards Towan Head in Newquay.
(c) Author's Collection (30 July 2019)
Top Right: Fistral Beach in Newquay famed for its surfing.
(c) Author's Collection (26 July 2020)
Bottom Left: View across Newquay from near Newquay Harbour.
(c) Author's Collection (26 July 2020)
Bottom Right: Newquay Harbour with the Atlantic Hotel up above.
(c) Author's Collection (27 July 2020)

p134
Photo: Fantastic view of Looe with its ancient stone bridge at its heart.
(c) Author's Collection (1 Aug 2018)

p135 Photo Montage:
Top Left: Looe at the mouth of the river with its quays.
(c) Author's Collection (1 Aug 2015)
Top Right: Looe beach by the river mouth.
(c) Author's Collection (1 Aug 2015)
Bottom Left: Looe with its bustling quays on the riverfront from the bridge.
(c) Author's Collection (1 Aug 2015)
Bottom Right: View inland at Looe from on the bridge with the station to the right.
(c) Author's Collection (1 Aug 2015)

p138 Photo Montage:
Top Left: Padstow Harbour.
(c) Author's Collection (31 July 2020)
Top Right: The bus terminus and former rail station building at Padstow in the foreground with the Metropole Hotel in the background (now known as the Harbour Hotel Padstow).
(c) Author's Collection (28 July 2020)
Bottom Left: The Metropole Hotel (now the Harbour Hotel Padstow) in Padstow.
(c) Author's Collection (28 July 2020)
Bottom Right: Padstow Harbour.
(c) Author's Collection (28 July 2020)

p139 Photo Montage:
Top Left: River Camel and Padstow Harbour from the Metropole Hotel looking seawards.
(c) Author's Collection (31 July 2018)
Top Right: River Camel and Padstow Harbour from the Metropole Hotel looking inland.
(c) Author's Collection (31 July 2018)
Bottom Left: Padstow Harbour with the Metropole Hotel in the background.
(c) Author's Collection (31 July 2018)
Bottom Right: The beautiful River Camel looking towards the sea.
(c) Author's Collection (14 July 2016)

p140 Photo Montage:
Top Left: The beautiful River Camel at Padstow.
(c) Author's Collection (14 July 2016)
Top Right: The River Camel looking across towards Rock.
(c) Author's Collection (14 July 2016)
Bottom Left: View of Padstow from the War Memorial.
(c) Author's Collection (14 July 2016)
Bottom Right: Padstow Harbour.
(c) Author's Collection (14 July 2016)

p141
Photo: Beautiful view of Padstow Harbour with the bulk of the Metropole Hotel dominant to the right.
(c) Author's Collection (3 Aug 2018)

p144
Photo: The Lizard Lighthouse and Visitor Centre.
(c) Author's Collection (26 July 2022)

p145
Photo: The Lizard.
(c) Author's Collection (26 July 2022)

p147
Photo: Land's End.
(c) Author's Collection (30 July 2022)

p148
Photo: Longships Lighthouse off the coast at Land's End with the vast expanse of the Atlantic beyond.
(c) Author's Collection (30 July 2022)